Swagger
& Sweat

WARREN BERGEN

Published by Jasper Island Media Ltd
This edition published in 2013 by Jasper Island Media Ltd.

10 9 8 7 6 5 4 3 2 1

Copyright © Jasper Island Media Ltd., 2013

www.warrenbergen.com

ISBN-13: 978-0-9880588-1-1 (ebk)
ISBN-13: 978-0-9880588-0-4 (paperback)
ISBN-10:0988058812

This book is dedicated to the entrepreneurs
who wrestle the future and bring it to us

CONTENTS

AUTHOR'S NOTE

It ought to be understood that the ideas contained herein are opinion-based, the result of personal experience, being witness to and having involvement in many deals, and an education of many mistakes and being guided to do some things right. The ideas are also the result of the expertise and experience of a great collection of many terrific, quality people that have taught, helped, mentored and contributed to the subject. Keep in mind that while some elements are straightforward hard and fast rules of the world, there are many elements that have had to be generalized in trade for the benefit of brevity. That said, while there are almost always exceptions to the stated rules and suggestions, the guidelines provided will certainly raise your level of preparedness beyond the vast majority of entrepreneurs with whom you will compete for investment capital.

Tom, related characters and companies are fictional. Several examples and stories are included in this book reflecting experiences and observations of the author, however, names have been changed to protect identities, situations have been altered or industries modified. Because all representations have been altered, the stated situations and characters that closely resemble real world individuals or companies are purely coincidental.

Additionally, be certain to seek proper business, financial and legal counsel prior to raising capital.

Regarding Gender

Within the context of this book, references to investors, venture capitalists and entrepreneurs are commonly cited as he and him. Certainly, we are all well aware that many great investors and entrepreneurs are women. The references are intended to encompass all equally and was only written in this manner in the interest of simplicity as opposed to awkward phrasings of he/she or her/him.

Book Format

The author has attempted to cover a variety of issues related to raising capital for entrepreneurs new to the effort. To further illustrate each element, The Tale of Tom is a fictional tale that reveals its story alongside the issues contained herein. At the end of the book are contributions from investors, venture capitalists and other subject matter experts who offer further insight on the many matters relevant to entrepreneurship and raising start-up capital.

ACKNOWLEDGMENTS

Rather than shine a light upon forgetfulness and selective memory, I'll direct my thanks towards the many that took the time to contribute, review, and edit. You know who you are. And thank you, dear reader. You are likely an entrepreneur, without whom nothing would happen. I'd also like to thank my wife and kids. You are everything.

1 THE TALE OF TOM

The Lure of Entrepreneurship Swings a Shiny Hook

Tom gripped the handset tightly in his fist, grimaced, and let it drop back to its cradle. His monitor clock showed 4:37pm. His left hand dove into his pocket for a quick look at his cell. Yes, it was on. No messages. Getting up, he looked out his second floor office window. Staring blankly across the parking lot and oblivious to the stream of those with weekend plans, Tom thought back to the first meeting. He wanted desperately to go into the weekend with news. Hopefully, with good news. Good news meant so much more than just the obvious impact to the company. Just to go home and tell his wife that the months of stress had come to an end. Of course, even this was only a temporary stress holiday, but Tom wouldn't know that. Not yet. They'd all go out to dinner, have some wine and hopefully, for the first time in weeks, slip into a solid eight hours sleep. Considering bad news carried such weight of consequence, it had simply become too upsetting to even ponder.

The pitch had been polished, practiced, rewritten and perfected until he could perform a solid cash dance at any time for anyone. The business plan for Titan Coatings was pretty good. Not too heavy on product, but highlighting the market pain, emphasizing a structured roll-out to a large and ready market, following in with management team experience and initial customer response. The questions had mostly been routine but increasingly thorough. A good sign. It had gone very well.

The pitch was always the fun part. Short-term excitement was much easier to raise than the long tough haul through due diligence to the finish line of venture capital. Getting to yes. The due diligence process had been a long struggle of seemingly endless requests for information, documentation and supporting data. More than three months had passed since that first meeting. Today was the day. The VC had promised an answer by the end of the day. An offer or a No. Friday.

Nine months earlier Tom and his partners had decided to pursue venture capital to fund expansion when banks either could not or would not come through. Tom volunteered to take on the job. Sales of their patented industrial coating technology had increased rapidly since inception to over $6 Million in thirty-eight months. The team was enthusiastic, but a new competitor was a concern and the opportunity for expansion into available markets was going to require a significant injection of growth capital. After thirty-one rejections, Tom was a little less than confident. His partners had been supportive after the twenty-odd rejections, but patience was wearing thin. Directives had taken the place of helpful suggestions. Screw them, they should try it. Raising money can be very difficult. One area of relief was that his sales team had run surprisingly efficiently these past months without his support. Perhaps better. He wondered which bothered him more.

Tom cast a glance back to his desk. 4:55pm. A family picture came into view reminding him of yet another group he'd let down. Missed dinners and parties. A lot of time lost. Even when they were together, he often couldn't keep his mind with them. He had noticed that his wife had stopped asking at what time he would be home that evening. Since the beginning of the new venture, this had been a routine query during breakfast. Does that mean anything? This had been more consuming than he could ever have imagined.

They had been in fairly decent shape financially as the quest for capital began. The ramp up plan was working, but the strategy was absorbing cash faster than it was coming in from new customers. Financing inventory had been overlooked in their first drafts of cash flow forecasts. They hadn't anticipated a financing process this lengthy and now things were tight. They had recently postponed the expansion processes when it became apparent that, in the absence of a financial partner, the partners would have to take second mortgages on their homes to get it done. To make payroll today, the partners had foregone their own salaries as most of the payroll was again covered by withdrawals against their personal credit lines and cards. When it happened the first time, the partners all nodded fairly quickly in agreement that they would cover the shortfall. But now it had happened several times and the company had yet to repay any of these shareholder loans.

Tom saw the line light flash before he heard the ring.

2 GET PREPARED
Or Stay Home

Preparation prior to addressing the investment community is a must. This is an absolute. Lack of preparation will nearly ensure failure, regardless of any caveat of which you may dream up. The gentlemen who prepared to be a plumber by getting an education, likely has many more clients than the plumber who did not. The guy who "is handy" will inevitably cause a lot more issues than our educated professional. Raising money requires preparation, is usually hard work, and entrepreneurs are generally surprised at the level of effort that is required. The good news is that because most entrepreneurs do not adequately prepare, they are very far off the target of where they need to be to attract investment capital. If in fact you are prepared to do the work, you will significantly increase the likelihood that you will outpace the rest of the massive population of entrepreneurs and win the hearts of those with gold.

You may also find that by the time you have completed the preparation phase, you will have a better company. Many entrepreneurs find that much of the work that was required to attract capital was work that should have been done anyway. Nothing makes you study your business as closely as when you have to prepare every aspect of your business and the implementation plan for the investment community.

Most entrepreneurs have no idea that they actually even need to prepare. So while they masses of entrepreneurs produce the same schlock as everyone else, the point of this book is to help you find those missing pieces in your preparation to help you stand apart from them, the 99 of 100 deals that do not get funded.

Be aware that raising money is a full-time job. To be clear, I don't mean a job added to everything else they have to do. I mean, it's all they do. One of the team members (founders) will need to assume this role entirely. If you're raising a fair sum, say something in excess of $500,000, please understand that it will likely take 6 – 9 months to complete a deal (assuming you have a fundable deal in the first place).

So what is it that investors really want? When they look at my deal, which element will be most important?

This question gets asked frequently, however, there isn't a right answer to this, the wrong question. Try studying a combination lock, then determine which single number of the required combination of numbers is the most important. A great product or service, a great team, sustainable advantage, pain in the market, and many other factors that are considered are equally important. Get all the numbers right, the lock will open.

Open your word processor and describe your product, competitors, competitive advantages, customer, market size, management team, staffing requirements, strengths, weaknesses, opportunities, and threats. Finish it off with a sizzling set of sales projections and you're en route to the investment community!

All we've got to do is get in front of some people with money. This is so exciting, they'll jump right in. They've just got to see what this product can do. Right?

I understand your enthusiasm. Really, I do. I too was once a first time entrepreneur that believed that my company had the greatest investment opportunity ever seen.

The business plan and related documents are tools that many venture capitalists and investors require, however, in Chapter 8 I will also show you how a single page could be your great asset in selling your investment opportunity. Let's call it the *Show Sheet.*

But our product/idea is unbelievable.

No. A great idea or product, as a single element, is oftentimes virtually worthless. It's mostly noise. First, identify whether you have an idea or an opportunity. Good execution on a good opportunity is the elusive jewel. Of course, we wouldn't have businesses without great ideas, however, efficient execution and the associated joy of capitalizing on the opportunity is very, very rare.

Tip! - See <u>New Venture Creation</u>: Entrepreneurship in the 21st Century by Jeffry A. Timmons for more on differentiating ideas from opportunities.

An incredible percentage of entrepreneurs convey "attitude" about their company. Some of them actually ooze arrogance over what they are doing. Do yourself a massive favor and do not be this person. The reason they do this is anyone's guess, but generally this entrepreneur simply places a lot of self-worth on being in charge of a company. On rare occasions, arrogance is mistaken for confidence. Confidence is great, but something entirely different. Confidence comes with having done all of the difficult but necessary work that goes into preparing a company for a capital raise. Confidence is brief evidence that the entrepreneur is likely prepared to speak to an investor. Arrogance is a beautiful red flag for the sophisticated investor to turn attention to someone else and not waste time with this individual so very pleased with himself.

Keep in mind that investors look for the obvious cut and run clues that enable them to get on to examining the next deal. The longer it takes them to find out you're not someone they should be talking to, the more it raises the possibility that they are missing out on a great company and entreprencur somewhere else. And therein lays their fear that they are wasting time. At the outset, they are curious about what your company is about. But then, they have to start looking for reasons to walk away quickly. If you've done the work, you will not give them the reason to walk away. Time and timing are critical elements. Time spent on the wrong deal is obviously not spent on the right deal. Comparably, investments made at the wrong time produce a similar result. Time excessively wasted and timing played off-key, preludes the death of the VC.

But our incredible product is proprietary and patent protected.

Okay, that's good. Competitive barriers are important, but can you sell the product? An overemphasis on your product and you've raised a red flag to any sophisticated investor. For a business to work, product is only one of many necessary components. Many inventors have great products that will never see the market because their owners do not understand this aspect. Most investors would likely rather own the company running with the second best product on the market supported by the very best team.

But our market is massive.

Define it more clearly. What fraction of this market is ready to buy, right now? Then throw out the portion of that portion that can't afford to buy your product because they're too small. Then throw out the segment of that remaining portion that will always attempt to build a custom solution by themselves. Then throw out the portion....you get the idea. Keep paring your market down until you've got that market defined down to a group that you can honestly describe as hot.

But our team is strong.

For what stage of the growth cycle is your team strong? At what point will you experience an issue with management depth or breadth? How will you know? Maybe your team has experience managing a five-office corporation with twenty sales representatives, one warehouse and an average monthly transaction count of 100 sales. Is this the same team that can operate a twenty office corporation with 100 sales representatives, three warehouses and an average monthly transaction count of 700? What is your human resource plan? Work this out, like it is the most important thing you've ever done. What successful organization are you using as a growth model for emulation and learning? Make HR a critical element of your plan.

But we have no competitors.

It is often the case then, that there is no market. Do not ever make this claim. It's a mistake that exposes the amateur that does not yet understand all market participants and elements that become competitive forces impacting a prospective purchaser's decision process. Be concerned about the competitive companies you've been thumbing your nose at, but be more concerned about the competitors you can't see. Assume that somebody somewhere is making something better than the widget you have just launched. This market paranoia will keep you sharp, ahead and ultimately alive.

Forgetting the *How*

Business plan outlines are available everywhere. Internet sites give them away for free. You can buy software packages where you just need to fill in the blank spots with your text, charts, graphics and presto, you're plan is done. Go this route and you're sure to join the desperate ranks of the 97 out of 100 entrepreneurs that sophisticated investors get rid of as fast as possible.

The trouble is that 9 of 10 entrepreneurs are pitching the same business plan that all miss critical elements of cash raising preparation. If you live in a city of about one million people, there is likely to be at least one thousand companies and individuals seeking investment capital for their emerging company. It is a wearisome fact for the investment community to recognize that almost all of the associated business plans are exactly the same. It generally goes like this:

1.   Company A has a product that is unique.
2.   Company A has a market so large that it dwarfs the GDP of most nations.
3.   Company A has no competitors or the competitors that do exist are such losers that we never need to concern ourselves with them.
4.   Company A sales projections indicate that all involved will be enormously wealthy in three to five years.

They've patented the product, have a reasonable management team, a big market, and competitive advantages. Should be clear sailing. The first problem is that the entrepreneur rarely describes the *how*. *How* will they accomplish the sales targets as outlined by the projections? Most often, the description is limited to vague references of direct selling and or a few lines relating to a reseller strategy.

Entrepreneurs tend to leave out the *how* aspect to their plan for one of the following four reasons:

1) the business plan outline/template used didn't require it

2) the entrepreneur doesn't know how the growth will occur

3) the entrepreneur thinks growth is self-fulfilling or easy

4) the entrepreneur is of the build-it-and-they-will-come variety (yes, these my-product-is-so-great-it'll-sell-itself dinosaurs still, and probably always will, exist)

SHOW YOU KNOW

Show You Know is a theme you will see frequently repeated in this book. The investor wants and needs to know that you know the plan for 'must have' product, sustainable advantage, exit clarity, market proof, breakeven point, marketing/sales metrics, channel management, human resources, finance, governance and systems. If you don't know, don't try to pursue investment until you do. If you wait until you can show you know, you will have a much better chance of a successful financing and you won't waste your time or the time of the investment community. A proper description of *how* requires an Implementation Plan. This will be described more fully in Chapter 8, but it's all about showing that you know. Remember this.

Sales

You need to show that you know what kind of activity is required to generate indicated sales. What key clients are garnered and when? How many distributors/market partners/strategic alliances/agents do you require and when? Who are they? How does each of these relationships translate into dollars? If you simply describe the business as required by most business plan outlines and stick in a projection at the back you have not created the connection between plan and result. Without the description of market execution, the investor is left to wonder and speculate whether those numbers are reasonable. If you show how the numbers can be achieved, there is less for the investor to be skeptical about.

Operations

On the other side of sales activity are the operations required to support that activity. That soaring revenue projection is only ever achieved and maintained by organizations that sufficiently build and prepare to support that increasing level of activity. When are systems an issue? When will your company have major senior team issues of depth or breadth? When will we have facilities issues and so forth?

So why does this investor keep asking for more information?

Ongoing requests for more information may seem tedious, however, many times the requests are required because the homework hasn't been done. Of course, due diligence processes entail a significant amount of information validation, however, many times the sophisticated investor requires a seemingly long and exhausting list of "stuff" that the entrepreneur often views as a pain in the neck. Every time the financier asks for another piece of information that the entrepreneur doesn't have, is likely further evidence of a lack of preparation on the part of the entrepreneur to build the business. So instead of fostering the comparative of VC as proctologist, file each request as a learning of how to be prepared.

Business is Math 1st

A prospective client explained his business to me and, despite internal admonishments, I could feel myself getting excited over what was a very powerful technology. The usual preliminaries looked good. Seemingly eager clients, an experienced team, etc... They had done enough study to determine where their pricing needed to be. It all came apart for me, when I reviewed the forward financials. This company was going to run in the red for nearly six years, and when profits were achieved, they were uninspiring at best. To the credit of the entrepreneur and his team, they retrenched and more than a year later found a new market and strategy.

In math terms, this one now worked in the proforma. Step one was done. The good news is that they now had a path to pursue that had a chance. The bad news is that they had wasted a lot of time, resources and money on a path that didn't. Business is math first. The financials are usually placed at the back of the plan, but in every case, they should be at front of mind of every entrepreneur.

The lack of an implementation plan and the lack of a good financial plan are the two top elements that make most business plans worthless and the associated entrepreneur is usually not funded. Those that do get funding without these two elements usually should not. That investment dollar should go to the deserving entrepreneur, the one who has cared enough and taken the time to get these important elements completed. The entrepreneur who received the funding without these elements and still succeeded in business, likely wasted a lot of resources along the way. In this instance, the team would have been using a learn-as-they-go approach. This usually means that the entrepreneur spent investor's money learning along the way when the entrepreneur should have planned ahead, but didn't and the investor paid for it.

Using Spreadsheets

Do not create a set of tables in your spreadsheet program with numbers simply plugged into each cell. Do create a proforma that contains algorithms pursuant to contingencies you've identified, then note the contingencies in your section entitled *Notes to Financials*. As an example, on the Human Resources page of your proforma, you may have broken out management and staff by department. Each time you add an executive team or staff member, HR costs are not the only area of impact. Employee burden is impacted, telephone costs, computer lease costs, etc... Do this in every area.

Determine the impacts of each line item and create the inter-sheet and inter-cell linkages that reflect each relationship. Doing this will create a powerful what-if tool for your organization. i.e.) What if we sell combined 10,000 units with a distributor earning a 20% cut with four direct sales people and one channel manager as compared to 7,000 direct sales with 6 direct sales people and a warehouse, but without the costs associated to the distributor? Of course with this example there are other factors to consider, but it is a useful accompaniment to decision-making. Many scenarios can be modeled for best course determination.

I don't know how to create a proforma.

That's okay. Just get the help you need. You cannot expect to be taken seriously in the investment community without a good finance plan.

Is my growth curve too steep? Too flat?

This is often asked, but this is the wrong question. The question should be, *"Have I adequately portrayed how this growth will be achieved and have I demonstrated how the company is organizing to support this level of growth?"* Whether the sales projections created by the entrepreneur have a slow path to performance or a rocket ride to the stars is irrelevant if the description of *how* is missing.

Show you know from where the revenue is coming.
What key clients, distributor, agent, market partner, strategic alliance needs to be in place in order to create the level of sales activity indicated for each

period going forward? If these are completed, you have demonstrated that you know how the sales will occur and who will drive them. Not including the *how*, demonstrates to the potential investor that your projections are random.

Show you know what the company is doing operationally to support the growth. What are the key points of issue internal to the company's operations that are required to be addressed on a go-forward basis? When do these key issues occur? i.e.) Q3 Year 2 – Management depth issue: Hire VP, Sales, Accounting systems issue: Migrate to a more powerful system, etc... If these are completed, you have demonstrated that you have taken the time to consider all department needs of the company as activity increases. Not including the *how*, demonstrates to the potential investor that you have no idea what will be required.

Show you know that details are important. I'm always amused when I look through finance plans and there usually is no identification of costs beyond the most basic line items. Get detailed, it shows you just might be responsible with money. For example, most business plan templates include a single line item for insurance even though most businesses require several kinds of insurance. After general liability insurance, depending on your business and situation, you may need to consider key man, directors and officers, business interruption, errors and omissions insurance, etc...

Although the list is endless, another area that is commonly overlooked is patent cost. Again, the templates often allow for an allocation for patent expense, however, they don't usually make note of the realities of true patent costs. If you've patented in your country, and wish for protection beyond your country, further investment will be required. Ongoing changes to your product line will dictate that additional patent work will require ongoing investment. Also, don't forget to identify financial allocation for potential legal costs, especially if your technology or invention exists in a crowded space (lots of patents that are close). Your patent is worth little if you cannot afford to defend. Patent suits have become commonplace to slow an emerging company in the marketplace. Even nuisance suits can encumber your company. If another firm challenges your patent, defense is rarely inexpensive. Offence also can be a financial drain, when someone infringes upon your patent.

We'll get into the details now. I would suggest that you take your preparation seriously. Become investor-ready. If you haven't gone through the work that it will take to be ready, do not approach the investor. You'll likely waste the time of both of you and ruin the opportunity to approach him again when you are ready. Most investors will not be completely honest and tell you why your deal isn't ready. They know that this is a fight waiting to happen that can have no victor. Usually, the investor will tell the entrepreneur that this deal "Doesn't meet my criteria". They will seldom be more specific than that because it simply takes too long to explain to the uninitiated, what "investor-ready" is all about and the entrepreneur would seldom accept whatever reason might be given anyway.

Show You Know that this level of funding makes the most sense. Run financials models until you know every angle. Did you pick the $2 Million funding target because that is a nice round number, or did you pick that number because that is the amount that allows the company to operate at its full potential, without wasting financial resources? Be ready to prove to a savvy investor that $2 Million makes more sense than $900,000 or $5 Million. It all has to do with efficiency. The astute investor will test your thinking here, so be prepared. Don't think that a bigger document is perceived to be better than a shorter one. Be as brief as possible. If you can describe how the product works in one page, I'm good... and thankful. More information can wait for the due diligence period should we get to that stage.

A Note About Timing

Do not pitch too soon! I truly hope that this little piece of information will help someone from making an error that is made repeatedly and often. While running an investor network, I saw hundreds of deals and met with hundreds of entrepreneurs. The most common lament is that finding investment capital was very hard. They were right. Finding investment capital is hard and it should be. When too much money is sloshing around for new deals, then way too many sub-par deals get funded. They inevitably fail in a big way, making the entire sector of early stage investing suffer as a result while investors head to other fields to play. During the tech boom years of the mid-late '90s, everything tech was getting a look and too many deals were done. Bad deals were done and it hurt more than just everyone involved.

Venture capital companies are generally funded by institutions and pension funds. These entities rushed to fund new venture capital companies established purely to invest in dot com start-ups. We all know how that turned out. The resulting major disaster is that the good venture capital guys then had trouble raising new capital for their next fund because the institutions were no longer willing to play in the venture capital pool investing in tech. Also wealthy individuals were rushing to get in the game of investing into dot com starts without experience or know how. Many lost most if not all their investment. They too, as a result, refused to look at real deals thereafter because they went back to investing in blue chip stocks, real estate or whatever. The message here is that finding investment capital should always be somewhat hard. It's an effort, and you and your deal should be worthy of the cash before it is granted and before you even ask.

What does all of this have to do with timing you ask? The point is that you often only get one shot with an investor, so make it good. Don't pitch with an idea. Put yourself in their shoes and think about when you'd invest. Maybe the first iteration of the product is complete, proven and working in several installations. Maybe the customers are pretty excited about the product too. The team is complete and the remaining limiting factor seems to be cash. Now you've got something to talk about. You haven't been talking about the deal all over town and you've avoided the media. This is the first time the investor has heard the story. You're new, so you're interesting. There are many deals that the investors avoid looking at only because they've been over exposing the deal for far too long. Few investors will like a deal that has been flogged everywhere even if a few good things have happened along the way.

There is a young technology company that is garnering traction with major American companies. The entrepreneur over-exposed the company right from inception, so raising capital is very difficult for them now. Their story is old and much less interesting since every investor in this region has seen the deal at least four times over the last 5 years. If they had used their own money and some federal programs for the development years and stayed quiet, they would now be much more interesting to the investment community. Instead they raised money in tiny $5,000 and $10,000 increments. So now that they are interesting to real investors, the share structure is bogged down by a lot of tiny investors.

Time and timing is also important for investors. Consider a venture capitalist. They market themselves and put up a website. The website shows their phone number. That phone rings....constantly. If you were that VC, would you want to talk to fifty prospects a day or the one that was referred to you by someone you know and trust? As a result, they usually don't take cold calls unless they just happen to have time at that particular moment. Usually, they put investment criteria on their website so that only a more focused group will call or submit their executive summary via email. Also consider the timing of their fund. If they started their fund six or seven years ago, they aren't looking for a lot of new deals right now. They are working hard on their portfolio. The average venture capitalist is responsible for five or six portfolio investees. At this stage, they spend an enormous amount of their time working on these companies in order to help out and get a good exit and they are working on raising money for their next fund. Any calls they take now, only steals time from other priorities. This doesn't mean they don't want to know about you. Every VC wants to build a second, third and fourth fund, so they may wish to place you on a watch list until new money becomes available.

Use your own money first before you ask others for theirs. Also, make sure you have taken advantage of every available tax credit and program available to you before you ask for money from investors.

Media Attention

There is a time for media attention. Start-up phase is not that time, at least outside of quick-turn projects. I understand that it feels good to see your picture and story in the local paper. It does not, however, do you any favors that outweigh the risk. Why draw attention to a market that you are sure is untapped and a great opportunity to pursue? Someone with much deeper pockets can easily roar past your progress. Maybe you think that your patent will protect you. Do you have a big bank account to spend on the legal bills to defend the patent? Likely not. It also shines another light on your company to make you old news when you're finally ready to approach investors. The other element rarely considered by entrepreneurs is that product development will likely take longer than what is being considered and when they launch late, they now look foolish for having made the claim. Overexposure is something most entrepreneurs don't consider either. The investment community that sees the same deal showing up at investment forums and pitching at various events eventually gets bored by you. So be cool. It's a little like finding a mate to marry. The guy that throws himself at a girl, calls her constantly and seems to constantly hover, will usually find a lukewarm reception at best. Be careful.

Tom Gets Prepared

The partners of Titan Coatings slowly filtered into the boardroom as they did every Monday at the end of the workday. The meeting looked the same as the leadership team meetings of Monday morning except that beer bottles had replaced coffee cups. Jim and Louise flipped slowly through the business plan while David sat hunched in a blackberry prayer. Jim spoke quickly, while glancing at his watch.

"Plan looks good."

"Thanks."

David looked up.

"Sure. I mean, great job. So you're going to start calling some money guys this week?"

"If we all agree that we are ready. That's the plan."

"Good. Should go over pretty well with the investors."

Louise closed the business plan and addressed the group.

"Don't you guys think we need more of a plan than this one document and a telephone?"

Tom, Jim and David all turned their attention to Louise. Jim seemed a little annoyed by the comment.

"What else were you thinking about?"

"Well, I'm not sure. I don't think any of us have ever tried to raise cash before."

"My cousin got a bunch of money from a venture capital company with nothing more than a business plan. We've got a lot more than that. We've got a great business and a great plan. We're ready."

David got up to leave, but Louise wasn't done.

"I think there's a lot we haven't discussed. How much of the company are we prepared to sell for the money we're raising? How do we know what's reasonable? We always say that a buyout will be the exit for the investor, but do we even have an idea of who that might be? And who exactly are we calling for money? I know Tom has that venture capital directory and plans on calling some guys with deep pockets, but it seems to me that we should go at this in a little more of an organized fashion."

David had heard enough.

"Look. Tom knows what he's doing. Let's just let him at it for a couple weeks and see

what happens. We'll get to those questions when the time comes. Besides, I don't think it'll be too hard. Any investor would be lucky to get a piece of this company."

Comments re: Tom Gets Prepared

While this is an oversimplified illustration of what goes on, it is unfortunately pretty common. Little homework has been done, little preparation, and they are four people who haven't done it before taking advice from each other in a typical blind-leads-blind scenario. It is difficult to fault them. Because they haven't raised cash previously, they don't know what they don't know. Many of us have made this mistake and I will include myself in this group. Until you been through the process many times, entrepreneurs either i) hardly know where to begin or ii)believe that it will be much easier than it is.

When David refers to investors being "lucky" to be in their deal, we are hearing reference to a whole topic unto itself. There is a lot to discuss here. Of course, there is incredible ego and naivety in this statement. But maybe, naivety is sometimes necessary. The entrepreneur rarely understands the real risk the investor is taking in a start-up, but that's often good. If those who achieved the great accomplishments in business, sports, medicine or any other discipline truly understood the difficulties that awaited them in their quest, many would never have undertaken their pursuit. Will the investor be put off by the arrogance? You can be sure that some will, however, the investor should be seeking a confident entrepreneur. Confidence should be much more evident than arrogance.

You do not get repeat chances with most investors, so being prepared is critical. Among other critical elements, we will get much more into the details of these preparation steps further in this book, but begin with the following:

1.   Have your executive summary, business plan, implementation plan and finance plan evaluated by your advisory board.

2.   Listen to the advisors. If you're not listening, why do you have them?

3.   Develop your presentation in their various forms (See Chapter 10).

4.   Practice your presentation in front of the advisors.

5.   Practice the Q&A.

6.   Go back and edit.

The Q&A practice with the advisors and friendly investors will uncover a lot about what needs to be emphasized or addressed in your plan and/or presentation. Target your investors as carefully as you target your customers. Investors have criteria that they seek prior to looking at a deal. Make sure you are not wasting your time or theirs.

There is a very successful serial entrepreneur that lives in my area who takes on a very focused approach. He always has several ideas that float around in his brain, however, he never speaks of them until he knows which one is the one for which he will be passionate and which one has the highest prospect of success. If both elements are not present, he waits until the right opportunity comes along. When the right idea comes along, he builds the team. These days, he doesn't even make himself the CEO. He partners with someone who will do that job and then sits himself on the board. When he's finished all the work of preparation with his new partner CEO, he drops everything and hunts down the money with unmatched energy. He does go too hard however, as he tends to drive himself to the point of exhaustion. I recall one such effort actually landed him in the hospital the day after the deal finally closed.

3 FOUNDERITIS
And Other Fatal Diseases

Let me begin by stating that entrepreneurs are usually fantastic people. I love entrepreneurs. These are passionate, driven, exciting people who are motivated. They are builders. They create opportunity, make things faster, better, more efficient and easier. They create jobs, inspire hope, and motivate others to follow their dreams. Without entrepreneurs we would all be nowhere and would have nothing. The true entrepreneur is nearly impossible to dislike. They are oftentimes possessed by a positive outlook, a belief in oneself, and a burning desire to try things new or unproven. Entrepreneurs are today's adventurers. They leave port with a destination in mind, but no way of knowing the route at the start because typically they have not taken this path before and yet they convince others to take the course with them. Others are either drawn to the gregarious leader, the cause or a need to be part of something new and exciting and so the team gets into the boat with a few provisions and sets sail. If they truly knew the risks, the headaches caused by the whitewater ride that blasts along at harrowing speed in rock-filled waters, many would likely never leave the dock. But they push off nonetheless. These are hardy, brave souls! They will likely not succeed every time they castoff for distant shores, but failure is only found in never trying again.

Purity of Purpose

Examine your motivation. If you are in your venture entirely for financial reward, either change course or find another venture. Life's too short. Find a venture for which you can be passionate. When times become difficult in the venture, (and it will) a company for which you are passionate is much more likely to find its way through. If you find a venture that you find absolutely fascinating, you will be much better off. If you love it, you will be more committed, more creative and ultimately, more determined to make it work. If you truly love it, you'll make sure that all areas of the company are in pursuit of excellence. Your competitors won't be as committed. They'll take shortcuts. They'll have less energy. So you'll research more thoroughly. Your product will be more refined, more efficient, more everything. You'll sell more. You'll profit more. In short, passion increases the commitment quotient to such an extent that it dramatically increases the likelihood that you will win.

Venture capitalists often talk a lot about the passion of the entrepreneur. True passion will be infectious through to your partners, employees, channel partners, alliance partners, and even to the investors. Of course all other elements must be in place as well. However, passion ranks equally as an element to be factored into investment decision processes. Passion can find its way into the investor's mind like that song you can't get out of your head. And it just might fester there like it did for Tom on his way home from work, until they too take the bait.

But no one knows more about Cold Fusion than I

That is great. If I'm investing in your company, I would hope that the company has the world's leading expert. Your contribution is vital. But does this mean you also know more than anyone else about HR, finance, marketing, manufacturing and sales? It's amazing how many times we see the omnipotent entrepreneur. Anyone who brings a wealth of experience in these areas is soon cast off if their plan does not match whatever dream world has captured the mind of the founder.

In the investment community, we continually hear stories of the troublesome founder.

• The founder who will not allow the investor sufficient equity to make the deal fly, so the technology lies dormant.

• The founder who needs to micromanage, so the company moves in ponderous fashion.

• The founder who thinks everyone else is stupid and berates the staff, so the employees stay only as long as it takes to find another job.

• The founder who believes that because he bore the idea, that he shall always be CEO.

- The founder who relentlessly tells everyone that it is always raining gold bars, so all soon tire of the liar.

- The founder who believes his company to be worth a monstrous sum, even though it's currently little more than a business plan and some half-baked code.

Luckily for the investors, is that these entrepreneurs fairly quickly show their true colors and demonstrate behaviors similar to those above. The investor becomes suspicious, pulls the entrepreneur from the shelf and checks the tag. Ah yes, this isn't an entrepreneur that we'd want to buy, this is a fiefdom entrepreneur. The fiefdom entrepreneur wants his own company, but isn't mature enough to really build a company. They'll have a little business, get to always be King and that will be enough for them. They'll dream the big dream, talk the big talk, but that's all it will be for them. A lot of these people are just bad employees and can't work for others, so they start their own business. The business immaturity of these people disconnects the capacity to perform in a sophisticated manner and win.

Letting Go

Imagine handing over the responsibility of parenting your child to another person. You bore the child. You sacrificed. You studied parenting methodology. You were so careful to monitor that which they encountered, saw, and heard. And the child grew. The child grew into adolescence and became a good person. The child became strong, smart, kind, but limited by your life experience of what you can teach the child. We all want our children to go on to achieve much more than we have. So the investors or board of directors feel that it is time now to step aside as parent, and allow someone else to be that guardian and provide the path to what was once your creation. It is easy to say that you'll hand over the reins when the time comes, however for very many, it is the most difficult event of their lives.

It is very rare for this not to be an issue. The founder may want to be CEO always and if the founder can maintain an "A" performance, they should stay. However, the percentage of founders that can move through the phases of growth is desperately small. Other times, the founder may step aside in title only and continue to act in the manner of CEO. On several occasions, scientists have indicated that they want to remain CEO in perpetuity. In one instance, the PhD expounded upon on how he could effectively grow and run a $500Million corporation. This was despite the fact that he had never grown or run a $5 corporation. Amazing. Maybe the University would hire Jack Welch to teach in the field of neuro-sciences. Maybe he could speak Mandarin without guidance, training or experience. It's possible, but only because there is a lot in our world that is entirely nonsensical.

To say that founderitis is a significant problem is an understatement. Finding a cure for founderitis could possibly accelerate global technical progress more than any other single effort. Under the growing pile of founderitis-inflicted entrepreneurs who won't let it happen lies dormant technology so vast and incredible, the world would be astounded by its power. Behind the wall of founderitis resistance are medical advances and cures of disease, scientific discoveries, mining innovations, nutritional breakthroughs and solutions in alternative energy to name a few. Without founderitis, our world would have more cures, more fuel efficient cars, less pollution, more efficient food, cheaper homes, better electronics, shorter line ups at the check-out and better tasting soup. Examine any object within your line of sight right now. Somebody somewhere has a concept for a better one, but you won't get it because that particular individual has the disease.

The source of founderitis can be a single element, a variety or combination of elements such as inexperience, ego, suspicion, greed, ignorance and stupidity. Whatever the cause, the result is the same. The technology is generally not released to the market or is so restricted in some manner, that the true potential of market adoption can never be realized. Few, if any, receive the benefit of the new technology, investors lose money, jobs are not created and several people in and around the company stand with hands in their pockets, shaking their heads, talking about what might have been.

An individual I'll refer to as Great Techmind created a genius technology for media. Great Techmind was introduced to me by a good friend and longtime angel investor quite active in the tech space. Unfortunately Great Techmind came with an ample heaping of founderitis. Not yet understanding the degree to which Great Techmind had the disease, I introduced him to others who helped Great Techmind build, test and prove the technology. I then introduced Great Techmind to three executives. All three had long illustrious careers in media. Two were C-suite and between the three of them, their skills and experience covered technology, finance, distribution, sales, and strategic partnerships. He explained his intended approach to market. They explained back to him that there were better routes. He told them he was right, thereby dismissing their opinions, experience and advice. Not an uncommon story yet to this point. However, the real disaster here was that these three gentlemen were prepared to consider a wide range of involvements to assist. While no commitments had been made, they would have considered either advisory roles, team roles, investment, or most importantly, opening their address books. Imagine the connections that could have been made and the increased speed by which this company could have grown. I did not introduce him to anyone further. The company now barely has a pulse.

The most common utterance of entrepreneurs that have never built a company before:: "I will step down when the time is right." Translation as heard by the sophisticated investor: "I will step down when it's too late." Finding suitable leadership takes a lot of time. Begin looking for the new leader one year before you need make the change. Professional CEOs won't be drawn to a company in crisis, so start early.

Tom Takes the Bait

Tom's look shifted from annoyance to resignation as he stared at his buzzing alarm clock prior to quick hit at its top. He swung his legs out from under the blanket, his feet hit the carpet but he did not stand. He stared into the en suite dreading the processes that would ready him for another day at work. Louise rolled over and examined his hunched demeanor. She had seen this before.

"Have a good day honey."

I'm rotting there. It's getting harder to go in every day."

"So make a change."

"I'm not yet sure how, but I just might."

Later that day, Tom taps the shoulders of two co-workers and they meet for drinks after work. He finds out that he's not alone in his desire to create a new venture.

Comments on Tom Takes the Bait

On his way home from work one rainy Tuesday, Tom bore an idea. It festered in his mind until he felt confident that this was more than an idea, that this was a real opportunity. He read the stories of lords that have gone long into business battle and returned triumphant, riches in hand. Bill Gates. Jim Pattison. Michael Dell. Richard Branson. Stories of big buyouts and moon-shot IPOs. The big exit. *Why, it just looks so achievable. And I'm good. Heck. I'm really good. I'm certainly as good as those other guys.* Maybe Tom wasn't fulfilled at his job. Maybe he was bored, under-appreciated, or felt he was under-paid and envied the success of others. Perhaps he always wanted to be in charge of others or at least of himself. Or could it be that he'd always just wanted to make something new, something from nothing? Hopefully, Tom had found an untapped opportunity and would leverage his related experience, skills and network to capitalize on that opportunity. Whatever the motivating factor, Tom was a new venture waiting to happen. So when the idea was cast and came into clear view, Tom leapt and took the bait.

Tom worked at Index Coatings for nearly six years. He had started in the lab as an engineer and had always impressed his superiors with his work ethic and intelligence. The company used a unique electromagnetic process for adhering the durable coating to most metal surfaces. He was moved into a lead role in production where he became extremely valuable to the company. From the outside Tom's life looked pretty good. He was earning decent money and held a secure position. But Tom wanted more. It became evident to Tom that upward mobility in the company was going to be limited as it was family owned and operated. He also learned that he increasingly desired to control his own schedule. After uncovering a developing market niche, Tom started to think about going out on his own.

What Tom has not considered is that perhaps his current employer might consider listening if they were aware of the extent of his motivation. Start-ups are very hard and the odds of success are not good. Not that this is the better way to go, but as each opportunity needs to be examined independently, an option here could be to create a new division within the company. Tom could run with the niche opportunity and utilize that infrastructure, financial resources and credibility of the established company. This option is not always possible or feasible, however, it is an option that could be considered much more often.

Tom has not exhibited the signs of founderitis common to many entrepreneurs, so we instead have examined his motivations which seem reasonable. He has industry experience, seems motivated, has uncovered an opportunity and understands that he needs help. All in all, good elements to a start are in place.

Often entrepreneurs are drawn in to take the bait for reasons that are entirely wrong. Check yourself against the following:

1.   Not liking your job is not reason enough to start a company.

2.   If you're the technician with the brilliant invention, do you believe that the hard part is done and the business stuff will fall into place as a result of the incredible technology and/or opportunity?

3.   Do you believe that the valuation of your business should be elevated because your opportunity is "special"?

4.   Do you own a patent which is licensed to a company in which the investors are to place their capital?

5.   Have you recruited the best people for the critical positions? Or did you recruit your family, friends or yes men?

6.   Are you willing to let them do their job in a manner differing from yours?

7.   Have you repeatedly found yourself hiring someone new, raving about their abilities and then six months later criticizing their every move?

8.   Have you ever caught yourself thinking or worse, saying that you have no competition?

9.   Do you have people with successful start-up experience either on the team or part of your advisory board?

10.   Are you able to listen to these people? Really? Have you implemented their recommendations?

11.   You have set up the performance expectations for everyone else. Has it been done for you as well?

12.   When the time comes, are you going to be able to step away from the leadership role?

4 ON SHOULDERS OF GIANTS
Be the Grateful, Happy Idiot

The importance of management excellence has become so important to the investment community that after reading the Executive Summary portion of the business plan, most investors and analysts flip directly to the descriptions of the management team. Evidence of a less than sterling team is sufficient reason to toss the plan and open the next. Many zippy technologies have gone unfunded because the financiers could not convince themselves that the team was bankable, that they could pull it off and execute the high growth plan.

The venture capital community has its own cliché of this aspect of deal evaluation and selection.

"We'd rather back an "A" team with a "B" product than a "B" team with an "A" product."

Translation: Superstars can do more with lackluster innovation than the lesser skilled with a product sensation. Once more with feeling, great teams get funded. This is not to say that a great team with a bad valuation, concept, path to market, competitive advantage or investment opportunity will get funded. It is to say that a great team will, in addition to having the right experience, often not make these mistakes.

Investors learn to spot a great team or hire others to study the team. They are looking for world class talent. Find it if you don't have it, but don't claim to have it when you don't. Due to the squander of billions in the Internet wonder years, to the squadrons of executives sent packing for financial misuse, abuse and fraud, investors are becoming much more diligent in their examination of management. Many venture capitalists utilize the services of human resource experts who will spend upwards of 50-100 hours of due diligence on the key members of the team. An emerging company really is nothing more than its people, so it makes perfect sense that the people are held to a tremendous amount of scrutiny.

Look inside your company and identify which positions are absolutely critical. Normally, it is the usual suspects of the C-Suite. Identify your critical positions. Now here is a very difficult task. You will need to identify the weak spots in the team. Don't try to hide them or try to convince yourself that the members are better than they are. This can be tremendously difficult as you'll have to ask yourself a series of hard questions regarding each position. Maybe some, most or all of the members are not "A" players. If not, be prepared to change the team. If you obtain funding prior to upgrading the team, make the change as soon as possible or else money and time will be wasted. If funding is difficult to obtain, it may be due to investor recognition of a "B" team. Agreement to prospective investors that you are willing to make necessary changes and/or step aside yourself when benchmarks are missed, are good selling points to your investment opportunity.

If you have a great management team member, state the background in solid, honest terms. If you are not a management team member with a great background, be honest and do not puff the profile or resume. They'll find out if you do and then you're done. Lying is almost always a beautifully decorated pathway to regret.

If you are the greatest CEO that ever lived, you will hire people who are much better than you. Who you hire will more directly impact your probability of success than any other element.

Tip! Read *Who: The A Method for Hiring*, by Geoff Smart & Randy Street.

If you want to know more about how to hire to apply positive impact to your company, read their book. If you doubt this statement regarding the criticality of the hiring, you really need to read the book before you do anything else.

So let's define an "A" team here. Each critical position for the team needs to have its description defined right down to each element of performance measure. Take a look though each member and see if past experience and skills match the requirement within each position. Now take a look and see if this person has experience in this phase of the business growth cycle. Cycle experience is just as important as a proper skills match. A zero to $10MM VP Sales is generally wired differently than a $100MM to $500MM VP Sales. Why? The person who gravitates to the ground floor opportunity is oftentimes attracted to the "wild west" of it all. They love the small team that becomes a brotherhood on a mission. They love the action of getting a buyer to sign on with a tiny company with a new idea. They love the freedom of the small company with a dream, blue sky opportunity and the openness of hearing everyone on the team. They love that most times, these young companies are not process heavy and that they often have significant latitude in their new role. Bureaucracy is as rare as a human resources manual. Examples are just as easily described for CEOs, CFOs and every other person in the company. We all have our comfort zone and it is an extremely rare individual who can scale with the company and remain a top performer. Most entrepreneurs believe themselves to be that rare individual.

So engage a team that's experienced for the growth phase you are in. The Senior VP of Sales from a multi-billion corporation will likely not be the right person for the job when you are still looking for your first million in sales. Also, the type of people who love the hunt in developing new markets for your tiny company may not be the folks you need when your corporation has entered new phases of growth. Identify key benchmark indicators in the forward growth of the company where each executive team member will be required to perform beyond their level of experience.

Of course every team member will have the opportunity to rise to the new challenges brought upon by growth. However, if after six months it is evident that the team member cannot keep pace with growth of the company, it is time to replace that individual with someone better equipped to perform at this new level. Continuing to retain "A" class team members is absolutely pivotal to the ongoing success of the firm. The sophisticated investor understands this better than anyone. Keep a ready group of "A" team players in your network that fit the next growth phase of your company. Try to keep in touch with at least five people relevant to each key team position. This way, if a team member leaves unexpectedly or it's time to replace a member, the process of candidate selection has long been underway. Much less stress for you, much more intelligent planning to demonstrate to your prospective investor.

So try this, be the idiot. You started the company and now you're the CEO. Hire people so spectacularly brilliant that you marvel at their intelligence, capability and performance every single day that you drive home from work. Perhaps you now feel beneath them and wonder if they know it too. When you achieve this realization that you are the village idiot amidst capable giants, allow me to be the first to offer congratulations for being a world class CEO. The greatest leaders in the world surround themselves with people much better than themselves and then allow them the freedom to do their jobs. At this point, you are providing the guidance, direction and end game vision. Let them bring it to you.

But this team is the team that will have helped me make something from nothing. How can I even think of replacing them?

There are a few things going on in this mindset. First, there is an obvious and seemingly reasonable sense of loyalty to a team that created the company from which they are now required to exit. Also, there is a fear that these people are irreplaceable. It's not an uncommon perception, but it is rarely an accurate depiction of the true state of the company.

First let's deal with the loyalty issue. Imagine for a moment that the first stage of corporate development is where those individuals really shine. You provided them with an opportunity to perform in a stage in which they perform well and they were paid to do so. People generally like to do well and tend to be happier when they are performing well. But keep them around into stages where they are beyond their level of ability and they'll grow to dislike their position and the company because the environment is no longer fun for them. They won't blame themselves, they'll blame you. You made changes. More people were brought on, so they don't get to do six jobs. You used to have more one on one time with this person and they thrived under your constant appreciation for everything they did. They went way outside their job description and did whatever they had to do to make sure that things moved along. You really appreciated the effort and gave them positive feedback as a result. Now there are a few dozen employees and the star isn't making Sunday night runs to the office supply store because the star knows that Monday morning the photocopy machine is going to be running at fine because *office supplies is now managed by "New Person" who always parks in my spot*. At one time they felt like they were the glue to the whole company and they loved the feeling of indispensability. They now have a fixed role and a job description. There's reporting and accountability. So now you have negativity in the environment. Nice job. Your intention of loyalty has now impacted the growth of the company, their happiness and the effectiveness of those around them in the company.

That one-time star now starts coming in late to work instead of early. Maybe leaves early instead of late. The former star becomes less creative, loses the sense of urgency, or becomes the company critic and dampens the enthusiasm of others. This type of person will always be happiest and most effective in early stage company development or in a small business that will never grow. This person needs the "family" atmosphere that is easily achieved in the beginning. They need the constant love and attention the founders can give when there are only a few employees. They like that they get to perform multiple job functions and the feeling that the place would fall apart without them. It's important to highlight this personality type only because I've seen it happen in so many companies that I believe that there is a real trend here that needs to be watched for and dealt with before it becomes damaging. Most early stage companies have one or two of these people who become an issue when growth occurs. Owners often give these stars stock or stock options and it is often fairly messy at separation.

The caveat here, of course, is that if the star is able to rise to increasing responsibility with "A" level performance, you have a gem. This then, is the one you promote and keep. These gems are the kind of people that will build a great company. They will be more creative than you might expect and achieve more than you imagined they might. With enough of this caliber of individual and you just might have a great company on your hands, because at the end of the day, your company's only worth is likely its people. An emerging company will always fall short of its value if your employees are "B" grade or less.

The second issue is related to a responsibility you accepted when you took that first check from an investor. If your company is financed by you alone, go ahead and keep the team to whom you feel beholden. However, if you've managed to attract outside investment, you're responsible to those investors to act in the best interest of the corporation's profitability and well-being. Your responsibility is now to maximize the opportunity and profitability of the firm and any personal agendas beyond that responsibility need to be left behind. Maybe one or more of those core team members will always be with the firm through all stages of growth because these people just seem to be able to rise to each new challenge. It's not impossible. Of course you wouldn't replace such stars. However, if people that were "A" performers in growth stage 2, are not keeping pace in growth stage 3, it is for the benefit of the investor, the company, the individual and everyone else in the firm, that the individual is replaced or reallocated. If you do not take the appropriate action and either help this employee re-attain "A" level performance, or move them out of their position, you are now acting against the company and now it is you that must be dealt with.

But I have family members on the team. How can I fire (insert name of relative here)?

This comes up a lot. Most investors are very sensitive to nepotism. If the investor sees a CEO who is husband/wife/father/aunt/whatever to the persons holding a position that is defined to be a critical position for the organization, he/she knows that it is very unlikely that swift changes will be in store for the person of close relation. As a result, the person may fall to a "B" performance level or worse and the CEO will most often not make the difficult changes required. If the CFO is a spouse, friend or cousin, firing them becomes a much more difficult decision. Investors know that. Instead of having to coach the company through this added stressor, the investors will normally just head for the next deal.

The other risk in teams made of close relations occurs when family relations break down. Imagine the environment where marital partners occupy critical positions within the firm. A breakdown of that relationship usually creates more disruption than most investors want to deal with.

If the entrepreneur believes that this team is the company and that they are indispensable, this issue is slightly different, but the result will be the same. As opposed to the well-known Peter Principle, whereby team members are promoted to a level of their own incompetence, the growing organization outpaces many of its team members that have occupied the same position for a long period through growth. Develop the performance measures that indicate "A" level performance and what level of performance would indicate "B" level performance. As you move your company through the phases of growth, you need to monitor team member performance in every critical position. Great teams get funded. If you still have the great team that pulled your company through stage 1 growth phase and you are now in stage 3 growth phase seeking another round of financing, be sure that they still would be rated as "A" players. When pitching investors, show you know how important a great team is to the growth of the company.

So first of all, identify the critical positions within your company and look at your team right now. Now identify the stage of growth that you are in. Does your team's experience match your growth stage? Maybe Tom hired a former VP Sales from BigCo Inc. and his LittleCo Inc. is running on six people and a burn rate that will eat available cash by spring. If you think that person is in their right spot, you're kidding yourself. If Tom is now taking cash from investors, that VP is going to have to learn how to be VP Sales of a tiny company. This individual is now learning on someone else's dime. This will make the company move slower than necessary.

BigCo had resources for outside consultants. At BigCo, the VP had regional sales directors who managed the sales team. At BigCo, resources were never in short supply. At LittleCo, this individual is almost always completely lost. The same holds true for the CEO and all other VPs. Make sure your company possesses the prior experience of where you are now. When you absolutely cannot match the experience to the stage, be very wary. Identify the criteria that define an "A" performance and track the position. For those positions where you're short, enlist the support of someone whose experience matches the stage. That VP Sales can at least then be supported by the advisor. This is not an ideal solution, but rather a temporary fix until you rectify the situation.

Tom Builds a Team

"I've already got a few clients interested. Louise can do the accounting. I have already developed the product specific to this niche and know I can sell it. I just need you and David to handle manufacturing, distribution and support."

Jim's eyes flitted to a picture of him teeing off at Pebble Beach.

"It would be nice to lose these desk chains. I'll think about it."

"Great. Don't think too long. I want to move quickly."

"Is Louise quitting her job?"

"She'll keep hers and I'll quit mine. When I get home, I'll look after the kids and she can do the accounting work for the new company."

"So she'll be doing two jobs?"

"Just temporarily, until things get rolling. Then she can quit too, do the accounting from home and spend more time with the kids while they're still little."

Jim flinches.

"What about money?"

"Between the four of us, we've got enough to start production. I'm pretty sure that we can grow organically, but if not, we'll just find some investors to back us."

It was all so invigorating. He could make any decision he wanted and until others signed on, he had to check with no one. He had already picked and registered a company name, and had a design company develop a logo and website (unpublished for now). No customers had yet committed to buying product, but they would come. Louise will look after the finances, David can sell and Jim is a superb chemical engineer. We're on our way.

Comments on Tom Builds a Team

A few issues already surround this start-up. Let's assume in this example that none of these team members had signed a non-compete with their previous employer. Motivations are all over the map amongst the founders. Tom has a need for control that will become an issue very early on and Jim just wants out of his current job. None of these people have been in a start-up before, so there is no one to discuss the realities of what it really means to build something from the start and to be responsible for everything with no steady pay.

There is also a potential issue with Tom bringing his wife into a position. Some investors will not involve themselves with companies with familial ties. The issue is that some investors will not believe that Tom will manage, evaluate or discipline Louise like he would any other executive that would work for him. If Tom is the CEO, then even while the others are partners in the company, they still report to Tom and he has to hold the position of authority.

Some savvy start-ups get their first contracts before they actually open their doors. If the product is in such demand and the founder(s) can sell, then get a deal and prove it. This way, you're at least starting with business and not hoping for it. Incent the client with discount pricing or perhaps if the product isn't fully developed, they could either partially or fully subsidize its development.

Things to Think About & Act Upon

1.   Positions & Measurements - Identify all of the critical positions of the company. Outline the responsibilities and expectations of these positions. Identify how performance is measured. Be sure those that fill these positions have the latitude, support and tools sufficient to complete their job appropriately. Have an exit plan when performance is repeatedly below standard. How will you replace these people?

2.   Advice - Have you built an advisory board? Don't just pick your fans. That's almost useless. Choose those whom you respect, have accomplished a great deal, and will challenge you in ways that can make you

uncomfortable. You're not looking for pals, an ego stroking or a love fest. You're looking for smart people. Pick those who can provide advice regarding the various aspects of your business based on their experience. Make sure you've recruited someone who has built a company from nothing. What about a scientific advisory committee? Have you even considered corporate governance?

3.   Attracting the Right People - When the company begins to gain significant traction and high level executive support is required, how will you incent someone to leave a good job with a good company to join your company? You have a sale to make. If the opportunity is as good as you believe it to be, you should be able to find those individuals who are ready to leave their posts, even at reduced pay in trade for opportunity.

5 PRODUCTS WITH SHOCK
And Awe

Real Gains

The investment community loves a product solution built for a market seeking a solution. It is always easier to find investment for a mission critical "must have" over a "nice to have". Seek solutions that carry an improvement factor of ten. Ten times faster, ten times easier, or ten times cheaper. Lesser improvements, as compared to the current standard, will be marginalized when competitors improve speed, make usability improvements, or manage to reduce costs. Make sure you haven't built a product, which now needs to be shoved down the throat of the market. Make sure you have built a product that the market actually wants and willingly pays a value that is profitable for your company.

But my shampoo formulation is made with bananas.

A disturbingly large percentage of entrepreneurs are flogging business plans which describe often interesting products that don't have a home. A solar alternative to a candle may be an interesting product, however, maybe people like candles just the way they are. In other words, your market may not be searching for an alternative.

We once read a plan with a technology that would allow a process facility to cut one of the expenses related to operations by as much as 70%, which would have an overall 5% reduction over aggregate costs. Now, there always seems to be a fly in the soup of every deal. Usually there are too many flies. Investors pick the deal with the fewest flies or the flies that they can live with or kill. The fly in this deal was that the prospective client companies in this industry were in hard charge growth mode in a healthy market and making big margins. Cutting costs were not a priority. Market share was up for grabs. Speed in the marketplace was their priority. There was no living with this fly. Nor could it be killed. In some years when their market had matured, slowed and become overcrowded, process refinement and other efficiency matters would become more important. Timing. It's amazing how many entrepreneurs risk their life savings, refinance their homes and ask others to invest money in a product for which the entrepreneur has not yet identified or measured market need with certainty.

But mine is blue.

Me-too products, even if they possess modest improvements, are not usually worth funding when they are intended to compete head to head with legacy technology. The investment community seeks innovation that can be patent protected or possesses such immense barriers to market entry that patents are unnecessary. The instances where me-too can work well is when the new company finds an un-served or under-served market in a completely unrelated vertical or sufficiently distant geography. Witness WestJet, which is the no-frills airline that mimicked Southwest Airlines. The entrepreneurs were smart to study a model that worked and not try to compete against it. They simply copied the model and moved it to a region where Southwest would not compete. The investors were smart to choose an investment where their total potential for loss was maybe less than 20% of their outlay.

If a startup regional airline hadn't worked after the initial market launch, they simply had to close up shop and sell the jets they had just bought. Both the entrepreneurs and investors were on the same page on this. Here's the tricky part. Good investors know when to cut their losses, entrepreneurs should also be willing to get off a lame pony and find a race-ready thoroughbred. There are absolutely countless examples of deals where the investors continue to throw money down the hole of the deal in an attempt to save their investment. To restate, when deals do not go well and take on the stench of the walking dead, many times the entrepreneurs reconfigure the deal and commence seeking new money. This is almost always a delay of the inevitable.

Create a Kill Date

Do yourself a massive favor and write down a kill date as soon as you start. "We are selling x units or $x volume by mm/yy or we shut down or sell off the assets". In the same way that the team has a consistent goal in mind to build and sell, have a cooperatively agreed upon date whereby you will either kill the company or sell it off. Venture capitalists fund on a 2-6-2 rule. The rule of thumb is that out of ten investments, two will perform very well, six will forever struggle and the last two will be outright failures. The six that struggle are often referred to as the "walking dead". The companies have failed to hit the growth expectations and are either on a very slow growth path or have flat-lined completely. Often, these entrepreneurs believe that the solution to their dilemma is more money. What most of them haven't realized is that likely one of the two elements is the real truth. Either the team is inappropriate for the deal, or the team is flogging a dog. The sooner change is made, the sooner the frustration of no growth or slow growth can be eliminated. If the company is a dog, it is much better to kill it and move on and find your thoroughbred opportunity.

But my daughter loves it.

Like flare pants and floppy hats, business ideas often fall in and out of fashion. You may convince less sophisticated investors to follow you into the land of flash-in-the-pan gimmicks and catch-a-wave fads, however, the experienced investor probably won't see much value in a bobby-sock resurgence. In the tech space, multi-media was the big idea in the late '90's.

Security, storage, compression…whatever. Please. Do not ever create a business plan around an idea because it happens to be hot with the funders at the moment. Pursue value.

The hard part is done

Okay. The product finally exists. In the minds of many inventors, the development process is the hard part. There is often a feeling that once a product development cycle is complete, investors should feel lucky to be given the opportunity to participate in their brilliance. From the investor's perspective, this kind of amateur arrogance is convenient as it easily identifies that it is time to reject and move on.

We have to only attain .005% of the market

While not true of all investors, many investors seek a company that can kill the category. They are looking for the solution that is not another me-too, but a truly disruptive technology that will dominate the market. What can you do to your product/service, to allow you to aim higher? Can your company be number 1 or 2 in its market? Again, I'll remind the reader that exceptions exist, but if you're aiming at such a small market share, are you truly bringing real value to the market?

Sustainable Advantage

Often the entrepreneurs will say that the current market has very low barriers to entry, therefore, their company should do at least as well as the competing entities. Since they have little that is new to offer, they miss the thought that when someone does create a differentiation of value or a real disruptive offering that provides the 10x factor, that the deal is dead for everybody.

The investors will also want to see that your product has a sustainable advantage over the competition. Identify all elements that are your competitive advantage. Then create a contingency plan for each element, should it fail as a sustainable advantage. For example, if our input costs are significantly lower than our competitors, what is the strategic shift that you will undertake when one of the competitors succeeds in lowering their input costs to match yours?

Don't forget that most products have a life cycle. What is your company when you've either a) reached the potential of this product or b) found that the product will never reach the desired heights of success?

Is it Big Enough?

Like many of the issues described in this book, this subject could be a book unto itself. New technologies or solutions are created every day and decisions regarding their future need to be made in each case. Perhaps it fixes a problem for an isolated issue and nothing more needs to be done or thought about. However, what if your brother came to you one day with a chemical additive that allowed tires to grip the road in a superior manner? Do you start a whole new company to produce tires? Maybe, but not likely. Neither of you have industry experience nor do you have any network to that industry. Perhaps the better answer here is to sell or license the technology outright to a major.

Try to think though the life cycle of your product. Are there a series of products that naturally follow in behind the launch of version one? Are there adaptations to the product that would make it attractive to other markets? Can you expand vertically within industry or horizontally across sectors? One of the most common errors seen amongst entrepreneurs, as it relates to product, is that the product is not big enough to warrant creating an entire company. Before you create NewCo, first ask yourself if this is a great widget that just might fit well into someone else's company first. The deal that could be made with that company can vary widely and could just be your best bet if you do it right. Make sure that the deal requires BigCo to have skin in the game. They either have to make payment guarantees, minimum volume limits, or some other motivating factor that does not allow them to sit on your widget and forget it. Otherwise, it can be easily lost in the labyrinth of a corporate behemoth.

I've seen dozens of process improvements, parts modifications, additives, and great products that just don't warrant the NewCo route. You'll see entrepreneurs continually generating interest but failing to get serious traction because of the product's limiting factors. They often love their widget and I can understand the hesitancy to set a new direction when things remain in a semi-stalled model.

If you still really want to create a company around a single product with a limited market, the other option is that you do it yourself. A small company can be quite profitable as a family owned and operated business. Do not pursue the venture capitalist community, but get it done on your own. If you later find a new opportunity with a better solution and a larger market, the venture capitalist will respect your accomplishment with the first effort and be more willing to accept you as an achiever.

Smells Like An Acquisition

The investors will also want a very clear understanding of how they will get their money out. Are there obvious candidates that will want to buy you out in 3-5 years? Do you want to be bought out? This is one area in which you and your investor better have good alignment. If you want to build a massive conglomerate, can't imagine ever selling out and your investor wants a 10X return in 3-5 years via takeover or IPO, you are definitely not aligned. Chapter 5 will deal with this further.

Returns

Remember the return. This might sound trite, however, most entrepreneurs choose to forego any reference to this speculation. Of course we all know that it is purely speculation. Who can clearly see what will happen in the future? Still, a few models speculating this way or that shows the investor that you have the consideration to actually consider their reward for the risk they are weighing. Put yourself into the shoes of the investor and try to be as objective as you can. Would you put your after-tax dollars into your deal?

Is this the best use of your capital? Could it earn a greater multiple elsewhere without additional risk?

Be sure you do the math. The best venture capitalists earn annualized returns in excess of 30%. Sophisticated individual investors seek similar gains, but do you know the translation? Let's see an example where, for the ease of math, the investor normally seeks a 10X return within a 5 year period. In this case, the investors inject $3 Million in exchange for 50% of the company. Given a liquidity event, such as a buyout, the sale price will need to be $60 Million in order for his 50% stake to represent a value of $30 Million. Can you get comfortable with the idea of handing $30 Million to the investors at this exit? Early stage capital is expensive. Get used to this now.

Widget Me Gently

The professional investor will likely not become enamored with your widget. On the other hand, they might love your widget and while that will increase the probability of investment, it might not be the best thing for your company. If an investor is also someone you seek to be an advisor, they need to be emotionally detached from the product and the company. They, as capitalists, desire to multiply their capital and this usually only can happen when people build the company intelligently and act in the best interests of the organization. You, as entrepreneur, also desire to grow a company. Don't be frustrated with them if they don't get excited about your widget. You are supposed to be excited by your widget. They have their job and purpose, you have yours.

Ideally, however, you find a backer who is enamored with the opportunity because they know it well and have an extensive network in the sector. Their experience could save you from countless headaches and will likely open many doors.

Tom Lands One

Tom and David sat alone in front of nearly empty coffee cups in a boardroom large enough to hold a meeting for fourteen people. They had scheduled a meeting with Jeremy Simpson, General Manger of Torrent Manufacturing, a company that could be a decent prospect. A wall unit at the far end of the boardroom held various awards won by the prospective customer to whom they were about to present. Awards for Best Managed Companies, Customer Service, Sales Achievement, etc... The company looked successful and was obviously well run. David agreed that it would not only be good to land a decent sized account, but that this company could work well as a reference account.

"Good morning gentlemen." Jeremy looked at his watch as he sat across from them. "My apologies for making you wait. One of our largest customers had me on the phone. So what can I do for you?"

"We've launched a new company called Titan Coatings. We're here to introduce ourselves because we have developed a unique product specific to your industry. Our coating is much more durable than other products and we would like to schedule a demonstration."

Jeremy looked again at his watch.

"We would like to showcase the capabilities of our technology to your production people and the engineering staff."

Jeremy hesitated while his thumb played with his pen.

"Do this for me. Send me some information on your new product and I'll see that it gets to the right people. If they want to see it, they'll let me know."

David started to protest, but Tom cut him off. *"Sure. I'll have a package on your desk tomorrow. But I want you to know that our coating will result in a major reduction in returns due to wear. Our tests show that it also has a lower toxicity rating and cures more quickly than everything else."*

Jeremy made a note on his pad. *"Thank you for coming."*

David waited until they had climbed into the car. *"Why didn't you let me work on him a bit?"*

Comments on Tom Lands One

Tom realized that they hadn't scheduled the meeting with the right person. Jeremy had looked at his watch twice in 2 minutes and didn't react to the product's durability. The GM probably is completely unaware that durability is even an issue. The GM leads the leaders of each department and leaves the operations of each department to each department head.

Tom and David will follow-up and will get in front of the right people next time. The upside here is that when they do get in front of the right people within the company and they bring their findings to Jeremy, he will already be aware of Titan Coatings.

Now more importantly, we should examine what is important to Jeremy. At this stage of the example of Tom, let's assume Tom and team are still at the start of their venture. Let's assume that Titan Coatings really has something special. This amazing coating has it all. Compared to competitive offerings it applies easily, it's safer, it's much more durable and carries an aroma that reminds one of sipping pool-side slushy drinks at a tropical resort. So Jeremy receives the information as promised and on time. He is good to his word and passes the information along to the head of production and to the engineering team for assessment. Assume for a moment that everyone agrees that the product appears to be worthy of a look, now Jeremy has to decide whether or not to proceed. Why? Jeremy has been through this before dozens of times in every area of this business.

Jeremy will now need to determine whether or not to invest the time and money that it will take to assess not only this product but the people that are attempting to sell it to him. At various times prior to proceeding, should they proceed, during the process of assessment, Jeremy will consider the following:

Assessment Time & Cost - Every person watching the demonstration makes $25/hour. An initial presentation would involve at least 2 people from production and 2 engineers. At 8 total man hours, that's $200 just for a 2 hour presentation and demonstration meeting, never mind the productivity loss of taking them away from their tasks for 2 hours. If that goes well, they would need to involve people from the line, purchasing, receiving and put someone in charge of the assessment. This process could run up to 100 total man hours or $2,500 to fully assess, test and implement should they decide to proceed. 100 hours of lost productivity time and business disruption is likely the larger consideration for him in this example. Don't forget to consider the broader impacts of your prospective customers. The point is that for a product to receive an acceptable rate of market adoption, the benefit to the customer should be obvious and significant. Investors would much prefer to see your "must have" product over any "nice to have" product.

Supply Risk – Jeremy will certainly be nervous that Titan Coatings is a new company. He can't be sure that their production system is ready for prime time and he can't be sure that their order management system even exists. Maybe they'll crater in six months and we'll have to reconfigure back to our current process which will take more time and more money. Titan is an unproven supplier.

Relationships – AAA Coatings has been supplying Jim's company with coatings for over ten years. He has had many lunches with their management and their sales rep event took him out for a round of golf at Fancy-Cars-in-the-Parking-Lot Golf Course and Country Club. Steak always tastes better after a birdie. But never mind the perks. AAA Coatings has been a solid supplier. Supplier reliability is critical and will be a significant factor in Jeremy's decision making process.

The Bleeding Edge – Because it's new, certainly doesn't guarantee that it's better. The test data that Titan provided showed encouraging results. That the test data was third party derived made the results even more significant. Pursuers of new technology are often referred to as being at the bleeding edge. It's called that because people are getting hurt there. Maybe the third party data looked good, but like most new technology adoptions, most companies want to be second to adopt. Let someone else take the risk, we'll see what happens with them and then we'll make up our mind. Maybe the test data didn't account for different metal types, temperature, and humidity or if whole wheat pasta could ever taste good. Real world results often find all the issues that premarket tests do not uncover.

Jeremy and his team have a lot to consider. Hopefully, Tom and David are mindful of these issues.

6 GETTING OUT ALIVE
And Rich

Consider for a moment, why an investor might write a check for your company. Perhaps this sounds odd, however, many entrepreneurs do not go through the thought process of what it means when somebody writes a check and hands over money to a company. The entrepreneurs, in many cases, simply see it as the role of an investor to fund the dreams of the entrepreneurs. "Yeah! He gave us a check for $250,000, now we can build v2.0 of our technology. It is going to be great. When we're done, I'm going to see if we can sell some of it to the European marketplace, as the American markets didn't seem to want v1.0." This entrepreneur is learning on the investor's money, which is wrong. If the entrepreneur wants to blaze a new trail, that's great, but that entrepreneur best attempt such experiments with their own money. Once you take other people's money, you better be clear on your approach and execution of the plan.

To answer the question of why the investor might issue a check is clear. The investor provided $250,000 in the hope that $2.5Million might be returned. If this were to occur via buyout or IPO in a 5 year period, annualized returns for that investor would be in the 40% range. This is the target. By the way, IPO exits are only relevant if the IPO market is healthy. Don't promote that as your plan when IPOs are not in favor. Now go back to your proforma, does your plan look like the value of your company will be 10X higher in 5 years than it is today? If not, you probably will have a tougher time accessing capital.

Let's look back at the example of Tom. The good news for Tom is that Jeremy's company did become a customer and a number of others did as well. The company is growing quickly, but still needs cash to fund the growth. For Titan Coatings, growth requires more equipment, more space, and more people. Tom is currently selling $1 Million of product annually, is still losing $150,000 a quarter, but anticipates profitability in 6 months. They then find an investor who buys 25% of the company for $1 Million, which means they valued the company at $4 Million post-money ($3 Million pre-money). The investor buys common shares and does not take a seat on the board of directors. He likely paid too much for a 25% stake, his common share issuance will leave him in a powerless position and he doesn't even hold a board seat vote. In short, he's cooked. And yet, when markets get frothy, this is how a lot of early deals are done by investors eager to part with their money. For many, like Hotel California, it is easy for an investor to get into a company, but sometimes impossible to get out.

Investor 1 owns 25% and the founders now own 75%. To generate a 10X, or 40% annualized return, Tom and team will need to provide $10 Million back to that investor in 5 years. How will they do that? Let's look at two scenarios.

Optimistic Scenario

Tom will need to have grown to the point where they could be sold to an acquiring company for $40Million. At the risk of using rule-of-thumb measures, let's say that the company was sold at 5X EBITDA (Earnings before interest, taxes, depreciation and amortization). EBITDA, in this case was $8Million. If the company was operating at an EBITDA % of 15 of gross revenue, the company would have to be achieving in excess of $53 Million in sales. This scenario is how first time entrepreneurs usually view the world. It is usually how inexperienced investors usually get involved with early stage companies.

Real Life Scenario – Tame Version

Tom's company took longer to grow and needed more money than what everybody thought it would take (and this is almost always the case). I have never ever heard an entrepreneur utter the following: "Gee that was a lot easier than I thought it was going to be and it didn't take nearly as long either." So let's assume the $1 Million investment was not enough. The company later took an additional $1 Million investment from Investor 2 who purchased 50% of the company for his investment and took a majority of board seats. One seat for himself and a few for his friends so he could have voting control of the board. Not fair? It happens all the time. If the

CEO can't get things going as the board sees fit, they now have the ability to turf the CEO and replace with one of their own if they so wish. They could do this if things were not going to plan and management was not executing as advertised. Investor 1 paid too much for his stake in this scenario. As a result, the company finds itself in a bad cash position and is vulnerable to what offers are available. You can insert almost any excuse here in the world as to why the company did not perform to expectations, but to the first investor the result is the same. Investor 1, the first one to believe in you, the one who came in early and at a time when it was very risky, when no one else would invest in you, is about to get his ownership percentage crammed down.

Investor 1 now owns 12.5%. Founders now own 37.5%. Investor 2 now owns 50%, a control block, but is really not to blame for this situation. To get 10X now for Investor 1 is looking more difficult. The company now has to sell for $80 Million. Using the same math as before, to generate that sell out price, the company would now need to be generating EBITDA of $16 Million and sales of over $100 Million.

Successful investing is hard. The bottom 50% of venture returns are showing negative numbers. The top 25 percent of the venture capital teams in North America do not generate returns anywhere near 40%. It is a very precious few firms that can generate returns of this magnitude and certainly none can sustain this level. Return on investment for angel investing is a more complex study. Angel investing has been done for a very long time but has only started to become formalized in the last 10 years as angel groups have sprung up in serious numbers. While formal data does not exist for cumulative returns for angel investing, some work has been done by the Kaufmann Foundation which has been tracking performance of the formal angel group's investments and their numbers look quite good. I would venture a guess that the angel investors within these groups are faring better than other angels because these groups also tend to build in educational events and training to help them become better investors. The groups often share investment and due diligence information as well to speed the process.

"What is your exit strategy?"

At every pitch session, an investor will ask this question. Of course, exits rarely go the way it's planned but planning it out is always a better idea than just leaving it up to "We'll get bought out". The investor is simply curious of what the entrepreneur might say. If he or she gets a "We'll be bought out for billions in three years", they'll know not to spend any more time on this deal. The entrepreneur has just finished a prototype that he wasn't sure was ever going to actually work. He's just thrilled that he can show it off and we are asking about the potential for an IPO or buyout 48 - 60 months out. Still, because you know the question is coming, be prepared to have an answer. Preface everything. "Assuming that the IPO market is still strong for our sector......", or "Although this can change in a heartbeat, currently the larger companies are rapidly acquiring any strong technology in the area." If you begin with this, be prepared for follow-up questions around buy out valuations and examples of IPO success stories.

But the bigger issue isn't around the idea of getting bought out that trips up many entrepreneurs, it is the act of getting bought out that is entirely under-estimated by the entrepreneur. Many entrepreneurs believe that at some point, a shiny black limo will pull up in front of their office and Big Co. will produce a fat check. While some of these lottery wins do occur, they are not normal and should not be written into the plan.

A six year old software company was exceeding $20Million in sales and had been profitable from its third year. They had an international reseller network, although most sales were generated from one large U.S. reseller. The U.S. reseller asked for changes to the software, the software company complied and sales grew. More requests for change, more changes, and more sales. The software company was having a hard time understanding why an offer was not forthcoming. There had been discussions, but no action.

The problem was that the software company was doing all the work of development and support. The reseller didn't have to invest in development, the reseller didn't have to test and perform Q/A processes. The reseller actually was receiving all the benefit and advantage of owning the company without the headache of running it. Of course they weren't buying it. The founders were good managers and if the reseller would buy the software company, the founders would likely bolt. There is no reason to buy this company. At least not until the managers figured out the problem. At the next round of suggested development suggestions, the managers refused. The reseller was perplexed, angry and determined to be punitive.

After a lengthy battle, the reseller bought the software company so that they could control the development plan for the product suite. The point here is that it is not enough to have a good company. For this buyer, there also needed to be a compelling reason not to leave it out there.

Build your exit goal as early as possible. If you haven't done it yet, I don't care what phase your company is in. Do it now. If you have an investor ready to write the check, spend an entire day with that investor and build the plan. "We will sell Company by date for more than $X." The board, investor and management team should all agree to the stated goal. Everyone is then on board with the same plan and has the same goal to which they will all work. By not aligning everyone's interests, you have left a significant amount of issues on the table when an offer does come.

Tip: Read John Warrillow's book, Built to Sell – Creating a Business That Can Thrive Without You

Tom Looks at Investment Offers

Hargrove Peterson

Hargrove Peterson poked at an iron test strip coated in Titan's new product. This was his third visit to the plant. His questions all related to the product, so Jim had to be on hand at every meeting. Hargrove then picked up a chisel, delivered several glancing blows to the iron and then leaned in close to inspect his work. Hargrove had spent his entire career working in the sector and knew of the value of hard wearing materials. He was a field man who worked his way up the industry until he founded, built and sold his own company. He worked the field for eight years before starting his own company. He built his company up to annual sales of $50Million before he sold out. Hargrove spoke without looking up, still looking at the iron.

"I talked to Jeremy at Torrent. Says they like it. He figured they will use it through the company if no complaints come back from their customers."

Tom took this as a positive sign. *"So what else can I show you?"*

"Nothing else I need to see. You're looking for five million for 1/3 of the company. I'll give you your five million, but I'll need seventy five per cent. I'll need the chairman's seat and no check over five grand is issued without my signature."

Gary Pauls

Gary Pauls pored over the financial statements, questioning Louise about every entry past, present and future. Gary was an accountant who had provided services to mid-sized companies for over twenty years. He had some money set aside for opportunities. He didn't like start-ups but had seen several of his clients grow up to become significant companies and was envious of their success.

"Here's the thing. You'll likely make a go of it, if you can keep costs under control. That's my main concern."

Tom didn't know what to make of Gary. *"So what do you propose?"*

"I'll fund the company for the full five million. However, I'll set it up as a convertible debenture."

"Which is what?"

"It's a debt instrument that, in this case, allows me to convert to equity. If the company is doing well and it looks like a big buyout is in the works, I can convert to equity and share in the big payday. If the company continues to operate without a lot of growth or doesn't attract a buyer, you keep up the payments and I'll still get my money back."

"What if things go slower than expected?"

"Then you probably won't make the payments and I'll probably own the company."

"How so?"

"Our security agreement has claims against all assets of the company. Or, the conversion rate we've built into the agreement reduces your ownership to a minority position to us."

Howard Blight

Howard sat next to his lawyer and said nothing. He instead whispered occasionally to his lawyer who, in turn, relayed his client's wishes. The lawyer had exceedingly horrid breath and seemed to take pleasure in looking over the top of his glasses when he spoke. Despite the fact that this lawyer had no business experience, he made many suggestions regarding how the business ought to be managed.

"My client would like to take down the full investment of five million dollars. We will accept your terms of five million dollars for 33 per cent of the company."

Tom practically gasped, but the lawyer continued.

"We will hold you to your projections. If you make both the sales growth and net profit projections for next year, we will maintain our position. If you fall short, our ownership position will increase to fifty-one percent. In year two, should you fail to meet your expected growth, we will own eight-five percent of the company. This is an offer and not a negotiation."

Things to Think About

Before you ask anyone for money, determine now how the exit is most likely going to occur. Build two plans. Find and profile companies that have taken a similar path and show that you are taking a proven route. i.e.) ABC Company launched and developed an industrial coating opportunity. They sold their product through an international distribution channel and even sold out to the distribution company at a valuation of x. Most companies do not need to reinvent the wheel. If you're taking a path and "learning" on the investor's dollar, make sure they understand this before proceeding with "the ask". Make a timeline. If you promised a liquidity event in 48 months and the IPO market is dead and suitors have not yet pursued the company for a buyout, what is your plan B?

Which, if any, of the above investors do you want to partner with? Hargrove Peterson has a lot of industry expertise and respect from a lot of people in the sector. He could certainly open a lot of doors. Can you live with his terms? The accountant's terms may appear more lenient, however at what value could he convert? More than one management team has lost control of their company because they took on a convertible debenture that converted into a control position when they missed their performance targets. The investor changed the locks and took it over. Certainly, Howard Blight is a social nightmare and, at first glance someone from which to run. Someone who can't speak without a lawyer is usually a nut job. However, I do like the "your value, my terms or your terms, my value" approach. There's a give and take there that is missing from the other two offers.

Perhaps, a fourth option would be to go back to the accountant and to Hargrove and have them split the investment. Bring them each a matching term sheet for half the investment. This way neither will own a majority holding even if the investment comes with ratchets on valuation. The accountant could potentially solve the pending issue of nepotism and Hargrove could seriously assist the company. The smaller investment lessens the risks for each investor as they then have kept some cash back as dry powder for future cash calls. Each investor will also be a little more comfortable knowing that others are coming into the deal and that they won't be the sole source of capital when times get difficult. The information provided from these 3 investors is too limited to state which is the right way to go, however, the intent here is to show that you will see a variety of thought patterns when it comes to investment.

7 VALUATIONS & TERMS
The Strings of Our Undoing

A funding gap exists between the seed stage and commercialization. Often called the Valley of Death, it's that place where the research and development is usually complete, but the company has burned through its cash to complete its product. Now, running on fumes, the company is looking to launch its product with little or no remaining capital. For a large percentage of companies, this is the first round of capital that they have to raise from outside of the company's close circle of friends and family.

Example: Seed Stage Corp

To build the prototype, the founders put up $50,000 and took an additional $450,000 from friends and family. They spent one year and nearly all cash to complete the prototype. They sold a meager share of Seed Stage Corp to their close family and friends, who did not balk at the valuation because they were not sophisticated investors that understood the process. The family and friends were just trying to be supportive and they invested because they care about the founders, which is why it is often called "love money".

Although the sins of over-valuation were committed since inception, consequence begins now. Seeking to raise a $500,000 round of market launch money, the entrepreneurs gear up for a raise of new capital. They have exhausted their own contacts and they begin approaching investors through referrals, introductions and assorted networks. The entrepreneurs are almost always shocked that no one, of any investment sophistication, will pay the excessive valuation attributed to the company by the founders. Assuming all else is well with the company, they may get an offer from an investor but will often recoil in anger over the price being offered. *"But that valuation of the company is less than what our families paid!"* is the cry. The entrepreneurs often do not understand that they simply over-charged Uncle George and Aunt Helen. They reject the offer, the investor leaves in search of another venture to support, and the entrepreneurs spend the next six months seeking another investor. Wearily, either the entrepreneurs often find and accept a similar offer and are now six months behind schedule, or they find more stupid money to support the bad valuation and delay the inevitable day of reckoning.

Seed Stage Corp has a successful market launch and with the $500,000, they have proven that their widget has traction in the market. To grow faster, they gear again for a $3Million raise and this time they approach venture capitalists (VC). Given the volume of deal flow that the VCs examine, feedback is often blunt. Oftentimes, the VC will force what is called a down-round, which is a reset of the valuation back down to where it should be. Now the family and friends that bought and received a too small portion for their large dollars, have an even smaller portion. Naturally, the friends and family are upset with the bad VC and spend the ensuing years complaining about how the VC model is broken, are no longer relevant or that they are all vultures. The VC model is only broken for those companies that do not fit the model and lots of fantastic companies simply don't fit the VC finance model. Some VCs are bad, an exceedingly large percentage are not. Most are simply willing to pay a reasonable price for an investment. The VC sees hundreds of deals a year and the good ones know more about acceptable value than your average first time entrepreneur.

Pre-commercialization companies are difficult to value properly because they don't yet make any money. Pre-commercialization companies are then often valued at 1-2X cash invested. So if we use 1X cash invested for this example, an investor putting $1M into a company that already has $1M invested, would then own 50% of what is now a company valued at $2M. And I need to say it because it gets asked: No! Other than salaries, none of the $1M goes into the pockets of the entrepreneurs! It goes into the company. Companies that have commercialized are somewhat easier to value as the investor can begin to see how much investment is required to generate an expected net income. Companies that have only been in the commercialization stage for a year or two often see valuations in the 2-3X revenue range. Older companies with operating profits are generally valued by certified business valuators.

Terms & Term Sheets

Should an investor determine that they are interested in investing in your company, don't expect a simple yes to your terms. Sophisticated investors will provide you with a term sheet, which is their non-binding offer to you. They may allow some flexibility on some areas, but generally will not stray too far from their initial offer. Look at the following and decide now what parameters you are willing to live with in each case. This list is not intended to be all encompassing, but instead will give you an idea of what to expect.

Opening - The term sheet usually begins with an expression of interest and may request that you cease conversations with other interested parties while due diligence is underway.

Dollars – The amount of investment is stated. Investments are usually split into tranches often tied to performance benchmarks.

Use of Funds – Dollars raised by the entrepreneur are not without ties and their use is restricted to their stated purpose.

First Right of Refusal – The investor will generally request first right of refusal regarding subsequent capital raises.

Security – This is the instrument utilized for the investment. Preferred shares, common shares, convertible debenture, etc...

Voting Rights – The investor may request specific voting rights with respect to the board. The investor may stipulate a certain number or percentage of votes allocated. The investor may also request a unique class of votes which are specific to certain events, i.e.) buyouts, mergers, lending, etc...

Dilution – The investor may require that his ownership percentage dilute at a lesser rate than others upon future capital raises.

Dividends – Can be set up in a variety of ways or not at all.

The term sheet is negotiated and signed by both parties. Other follow-on documents are the:

Share Purchase Agreement – The subscription agreement specific to the investment.

Shareholders Agreement – No shareholders agreement is a template. This agreement is always a unique document, but be sure to consider elements regarding the rights of the shareholders regarding profits distributions, exits, IPO considerations, etc...

Legal Agreements
Once you and an investor have agreed to a deal, legal agreements will need to be created. You can save a significant amount of time, energy and money by utilizing a group of template agreements that have been created by a

team of leading venture capital attorneys. These documents are in the public domain and are available at www.nvca.org in the resources section. At the time of writing, you will find the following:

- Term Sheet
- Stock Purchase Agreement
- Certificate Of Incorporation
- Investor Rights Agreement
- Voting Agreement
- Right of First Refusal and Co-Sale Agreement
- Management Rights Letter
- Indemnification Agreement
- Model Legal Opinion

Get to know these documents. Read them and understand them. These documents are not a replacement for legal counsel. They simply provide a method of saving some time and money in the process. Additionally, these documents will provide a documentation platform that will minimize material gaps.

What about debt?

Of course angel and venture capital investment are not your only options. Lots of entrepreneurs are using home equity, credit cards, family and friends. You may even find the occasional opportunity to take on debt. But should you use it? Debt that is available for early stage ventures usually comes at a very high interest rate. Sure, it's non-dilutive to your ownership position, however there are other things to consider. Is the rate at which you are building shareholder value greater or less than the combined annualized cost of the interest rate and all associated fees? There lies part of your answer. If the rate of shareholder value growth is lower than the total cost of the debt, you would be destroying shareholder value by taking it on. But there is also the issue that any issuer of early stage debt likely requires that you sign personal guarantees. Personal guarantees can be very scary. When times get difficult in your venture and you fall behind in your payments on debt, they will come after you. In an effort to help you remember this little tidbit, let me tell you a story.

When Bears are Hungry, You and Your Personal Guarantees are a Ham Sandwich

There was a narrow but paved road that followed the curves of a long pretty lake. On the other side of the road, a mix of pine and poplar trees filtered warm summer sun onto their passersby. It was a beautiful experience to take this drive, especially by motorcycle as it seemed to deepen the experience as it all played along to a happy Ducati thrum. I had heard of stories of bears in the trees of faraway places and listened to tales of attack and consequence.

I asked them if they worried about bears in our trees. *No*, came the response. The route along the lake was very enticing and I began taking it more frequently and faster. Maybe I was enjoying the scenery a little less as I started leaning harder into its curves. Others were impressed by my times which encouraged me to further increase my speed. Some went as far as to promise a faster and more powerful bike if my times continued to improve. Maybe I stopped surveying the lake and contemplating the trees. Certainly there was a thrill of driving fast that had overshadowed the pleasure of the route. One no longer views the lake or contemplates the trees when the route has become a track. Then there was another attack. Not at our lake, but not quite so far away and it was a kind of bear of which we had never heard. Again we talked about the danger of bears and the possibility of taking new routes. Apparently other routes had now closed but no one had seen that kind of bear at our lake or in our trees.

I kept driving, although I have to admit that the appeal of this route had been diminished since the closure of other routes. Having options is extremely valuable. And then it happened. After just rounding a left turning bend, a large and fearsome form came crashing through the trees. The trees that held close to the side of road hid the bear from view until he was entirely upon me. I had just begun to look toward the oncoming animal as he slammed a branch through spokes of my front wheel. It's funny how accidents occur in slow motion when you're in them. I clearly recall seeing a duck flip under the water's surface as I flew through the air. With my slide completed abruptly at the base of a tree, I lifted my head just in time to see the bear hoist the bike over his head and smash it upon a stump. He ate the lunch I had strapped to the seat and ripped the rubber from the rims. It was then his turn to lift his head and focus his sights on me. His eyes were wild and raging. There was blood, still wet, on his claws and teeth. I will not ever forget.

Apparently there were many attacks at all the lakes from all the bears in all the trees. Carnage was common and widespread. I suffered through my attack, waited until he had gone and limped back in search of the man with whom I had previously spoken.

"There are bears in our trees." I said.

"Yes. I knew they would come." He said.

"I was attacked." And I told him my story.

"Oh. That's too bad." He said with a shrug. "That's why I drive a car."

8 STAND OUT
And Stand Apart

Obviously your quest for cash requires a package of documentation. Have the following available and at the ready:

- A Single Fast Facts Page
- A Show Sheet
- An Executive Summary
- A New Current Business Plan
- An Implementation plan – most critical!
- An HR Plan
- A Finance Plan
- A Marketing Plan
- A Sales Process Plan (each of these plans should clearly feed through the cash flow statements)

- A copy of each business, finance, marketing and sales plan created prior to the current one

- The Party Presentation – A 30 second blitz. Example - "I'm with Titan Coatings. We have a patented product for increased life span of industrial components by a factor of 10. We're operating at overcapacity in our small space and need capital to expand."

- A whiteboard presentation

- A PowerPoint presentation

An Executive Summary in Proper Form

You have two to four pages to cover market pain, solution, market opportunity, approach to market, management, capital requirements, use of funds and estimated event for investor liquidity. Write it, read it. Is it exciting? Compelling? Really? Write it again; be more concise than the first draft. Pull out the adjectives, leave in the intensity. Get the information across but be as brief as possible. If you can say it in 12 words, don't use an entire page. Brevity and clarity are your friends. Hand it out to some business people you know. Ask them to underline anything that is unclear. i.e.) industry lingo. Ask them for brutal honesty. If you are so lucky as to get honesty from them (many hate to be critical), don't argue. Thank them and later try to determine objectively if the criticism is valid. Do not expect your early drafts to be great. You likely haven't studied and written dozens of business plans. Many investors see over 100 plans a year. Like everything, revisions and practice allows refinement.

Don't forget that most entrepreneurs focus on their product in their executive summary and business plan. This overemphasis on product creates another opportunity for you to look and sound more professional that everybody else. Focus on the opportunity and the plan for execution. To many investors, the product is meaningless. It is merely the vehicle in which we drive the opportunity. Your proper focus will tower over the presentations of the others.

Now make the document look professional. If you don't know how to do that, find a professional graphics designer who can help. Take a look at other work they have done. If it conveys the same kind of professionalism that you'd find in a document from a Fortune 500 organization, you've found your help. If you consider that there are one thousand other entrepreneurs seeking capital in your city, you'll understand that you are now selling something in a very competitive environment. The investment opportunity is now your product and the prospective investor is your customer.

If you want to be the one in one hundred that gets funded, be better than average in all aspects of the business, product, team and implementation. Make your documents better too. Make your document read more professionally and look more professional. You should want to get the executive summary honed until others feel that it is so compelling, that those who read it will want to learn more. For now, that's your only goal.

The New Business Plan - Show You Know

Once you have captured some interest via the Executive Summary, the investor now needs to determine if the entrepreneur knows what needs to be done or if the entrepreneur is just another one of many. Again, shorter is better. The plan should be completed in as few pages as possible. The various business plan outlines you find are generally fine, however, build in an implementation plan to actually be informative.

Building a proper implementation plan provides a dual benefit. The entrepreneur is allowing the investor to identify that the team understands what needs to be done. The investor is looking for a clear and logical path from the current state through the next phases of growth. An entrepreneur that is serious about growth will build one whether investment capital is being sought or not. If one is not built, the entrepreneur effectively communicates to the investor that they need not waste any additional time.

Illustration of Titan Coatings

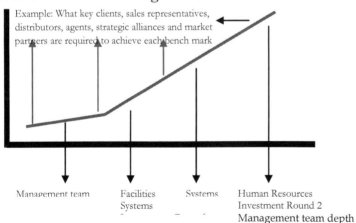

Example: What key clients, sales representatives, distributors, agents, strategic alliances and market partners are required to achieve each bench mark

| Management team | Facilities Systems | Systems | Human Resources Investment Round 2 Management team depth |

Identify all key points of critical change as the firm moves forward through the phases of growth.

When designing your implementation plan, imagine your business within the above chart as a place to start. It helps to think through the various requirements for growth from a sales perspective as well as identifying the operational changes required to support this growing organization. The examples in the chart are just examples and need to be altered for your situation. Every company will have its own list of operational major inflection points that will allow it to evolve into the next growth phase. The arrows pointing up are sales benchmarks. Make sure you have developed the marketing & sales metrics that will allow an outsider to understand how these sales achievements are predictable. For example, "We already know that we spend $50,000 on marketing to produce 100 leads, in order to produce 10 sales which brings in $500,000 revenue. Our marketing/sales metric is therefore 10 to 1 and our close ratio is 10%. When you can produce this kind of information, investors will stop smirking when they see your projections.

If the investor now believes that these sales targets are possible, they will wonder if the team can execute on the plan and how far they have thought through the functional areas of the company and what will be required to build a company that can actually produce and support this level of growth successfully. Therefore developing a plan for each functional area of the company for the demonstrated period for which we are making sales projections is entirely rational. Once you backup your projections with metrics and show that you have the implementation plan for the company, you will be very, very different from almost all other companies that are competing with you for those investment dollars.

The Marketing Plan – Driving Desire

First of all, let's be perfectly clear on the difference between marketing and sales. Marketing is the entirety of effort, activities and investment that is required to create a lead or prospective customer. Sales is the process that begins after the lead or prospective customer has been identified. The new business plan illustrates the power of your product, the reasons why the intended market will buy, the resulting opportunity that awaits your team and offering. The investor now needs to know how the entrepreneur intends to create interest in the product. Perhaps the plan refers to a direct sales strategy, but before selling processes begins, a sales lead needs to be created by marketing processes.

Imagine your marketing plan is an hour glass. The top half of the hour glass is filled with prospects. The processes employed and work undertaken is intended to direct prospects into becoming that single grain of sand that falls through to the bottom half of the hour glass. At this point, the grain transforms from a marketing prospect to a sales lead and sales processes take over from there.

Describe the following:

- How will your company get its messaging to the buyers in order to create a sales lead? Meaning how will you make your market aware of your offering?
- What activities will be undertaken over the next twelve months to create sales leads? Create a plan for each activity in a revolving 90 day

format. (i.e. advertising, cold calls, tradeshows, distributors or resellers, online lead generation)

- Who is responsible for each of these activities?
- What materials will be required for each of these activities?
- What is the cost for each activity?
- How will you measure the result of each activity?
- What was the resulting cost per lead for each activity?

With this information closely managed and monitored, you will be able to make informed adjustments to the plan for the following year. The adjustments will be based on working data and not just hunches and gut feel. With these elements in place, you will be able to intelligently answer the questions about costs of client acquisition, cost per lead by activity, etc... A lot of people are drawn to marketing because they think that it is all about brochures and a nice logo. Real marketing is hard work. A great marketing team with a great plan supports the sales team by feeding them sales leads. Investors will be impressed that you know how much it will costs and how much effort and resources are required in order to produce sales of $X. Few entrepreneurs bother to do this work. Don't be like everybody else.

The Sales Process Plan – Converting Desire to Dollars

Many business plans proudly display a soaring growth curve representing projected sales. The most common failure among new companies is an inability to recreate real world sales activity that was previously displayed in the chart. Understanding that this is the case, it is only logical to try to provide evidence to alleviate any potential skepticism.

Most companies create processes for every department in the organization in order for it to be effective and the sales department is most often overlooked. The result of a lack of sales process in the organization is inconsistent account management, inconsistent prospect experience, inaccurate sales forecasting, and inevitably erratic or disappointing sales results. Identify for the investor your company's sales cycle processes. By doing this, you will show you know how to sell your product. By doing this, you will have shown that you are prepared. By doing this, you have removed one more of the many barriers that exist between you and a positive response from a sophisticated investor.

Nobody will ask me for this

> You might be right, but the entrepreneur that is organized has a much better opportunity to remove doubt in the mind of the investor than the entrepreneur who is not. I also believe that most investors should be asking for this. Selling is the whole point. The company that can't sell is a dog. Besides, you should be doing this even if you weren't raising capital.

Create a sales process for your company even if you are the only one in the company. Modify the process as you work it, until you can hand it to your first hired sales person as a true operative guide to selling your product.

- What are the steps of selling?

- What materials are required in each step of the sales cycle?

- What are the corporate "permissions" within each step? i.e.) At stage 5, we are clear to expense up to $1,000 in travel to advance the account to stage 6.

The results of building a good selling process plan within the organization are dramatic. The goal of a defined selling process is to create, evolve and adopt a consistent, predictable, normal course of prospect interaction until it is a smoothly running machine. Prospect A is handled as professionally as Prospect B which is being managed by a completely different sales representative. The steps of the sale are the same, the materials at each step is the same. The rep communicates to prospect what will happen next and by when. "A package of information will be on your desk within 48 hours." And then this actually occurs. Each step refers to the next with a timing promise. By the time the prospect makes the purchase decision, they are more than enamored by you, they trust you. They trust you because you did what you said you were going to do by a specific time. Their attitude then becomes this: "They cared about me to such an extent through this whole process when I promised them nothing in return." Their opinion of you and your company is heightened to the extent that they then think, "How could their product be inferior, when they have been so excellent in every other regard. Their product is likely superior in every way."

Almost every company says "we compete by providing great customer service" and yet they do not have any consistency when dealing with prospects. Without sale process consistency, that "great customer service" motto is simply making themselves feel good and little else.

1. Consistent Client Experience

Most companies with outbound sales teams have a bad habit. There is consistency in all department workflow patterns except the sales department. At some point, Corporate America accepted the notion that selling is an art and process has no place in this profession. This antiquated view of selling produces the following team environment. Jim likes to take his prospective and current clients golfing. Susan likes to communicate almost entirely by phone. Jerry likes to prospect more than he likes to maintain his client base so he dedicates 85 percent of his time to that end. All prospective and current clients to the company have an inconsistent experience with Company A. All Company A representatives deal with prospects in a manner that is reflective of their personal belief of the right way to sell. What if we let every accountant create statements that are more reflective of their personality? *"Our office equipment is actually appreciating in value!"* Ever notice that most companies with an outbound sales team have a few high-octane producers and a herd of low-mid grade performers? Work the logical best practice elements of the winners into the corporate selling methodology.

The sales rep dominates the human contact your client will have with your company. If you can control the experience the client has with your company, you have a much better shot at generating the desired market impression of your company.

2. Shortened Selling Cycles

If you continue to build and refine the sales process, it is reasonable to predict that over time, the selling cycle will shorten. The team without a documented process is simply continuing to relearn how to sell their widget in a never improving pattern of behavior. Additionally, the new sales representative has a much easier transition into a company that can hand over a process. Ramp up time for this new rep is reduced dramatically and they will need to rely on help from other representatives much less.

3. Forecasting Accuracy

In most sales team meetings across the country, the team will meet at the end of the month to discuss results of the month past and provide anecdotal evidence as to how the next month will turn out. The sales manager takes these stories to heart and makes whatever adjustments they feel necessary before reporting the forecast to the VP or President. When results present a shortfall, the VP or President hammers the Sales Manager, who in turn, hammers the team members that are short of goal. Imagine instead, a simple report by the reps indicating the value and number of contracts by sales process stage. The forecasts are then modeled independent of "feel" or ego. The manager eyeing the rep without results generally assumes that the rep is not working. By seeing that the rep is working, but can't close provides an opportunity for choice. The manager can choose to fire or assist. The rep that can move a prospect deftly through the process but can't close maybe needs closure training rather than a termination notice. It's up to the sales manager, but at least the manager can see the activity.

4. Team Management

George was always the bottom performer. In other environments, George would likely have been fired. Process enabled the company to identify that George was very good at moving clients through the process, but a classic non-closer. By bringing in the sales manager to close a few deals in co-operation with George, he was soon taking the initiative in this area that had previously been a cause of fear.

A Show Sheet

If you take only one piece of advice from this book, create a show sheet. A show sheet is a single page that is the summary of all of the work and planning that has been done for the company and its opportunity. It is the extreme summary of the business plan, implementation plan and a resulting financial snapshot. A show sheet will allow you to meet with an investor and intelligently discuss the growth path of the company. The show sheet encapsulates the entire story of the growth plan and each cell in the table can be a discussion with the prospective investor. Discussion is good. If the investor is asking questions about each cell, the investor is challenging your thinking about the growth plan to see how well you have thought it through.

This following statement will, at first blush, sound like a wide sweeping overstatement or generalization. *If the investor believes your projections, the investor will invest.* There are, however, lots of reasons not to believe the projections. Team issues, competition, economic shifts, patent disputes, etc... But assuming all the due diligence has been done and everything is perfect the only real reason for an investor not to invest is that they don't believe your plan. So the favor that you can do for yourself is to make the first meeting as direct and simply portrayed as possible. Now, behind each cell in the table resides a lot of information, documentation planning and support. There is no other document, other than a show sheet, that can demonstrate the company plan in such a simple format. This sheet will go a long way in creating conversation with your prospective investor. It also works very well as opposed to just sending them a business plan. Unless they called you and asked for it, they likely won't read it. A one on one conversation is much better.

It is important to note that the show sheet should be done in every company anyway. Across the top, create heading for each quarter. Then down the side create rows for each operating department of the company including but not limited to sales, ebitda, inventory, marketing, finance, human resources, systems, facilities, etc...   This document should then sit atop the desk of each leadership team member in the company. This way, everyone knows what everyone else is doing and what they are to achieve in every single quarter. It's a great way to stay on track and very literally, on the same page.

Titan Coatings Show Sheet				
Benchmarks	Timeframe 1	Timeframe 2	Timeframe 3	Timeframe 4
Revenue	$xx,xxx	$xxx,xxx	$x,xxx,xxx	$x,xxx,xxx+
General & Admin	$x	$xx	$xx	$xx
EBITDA	($$$)	($$)	$	$$$
Clients	Startup Phase # clients Initial clients are covering a portion of development costs.	Start - Growth Phase # clients Financing is critical to this period. Company expenses are still in excess of revenue.	Growth to near Profitability Phase ## clients At ## clients, Company is on nearing niche clear market acceptance.	Profitability Phase ### clients Company is a well-established entity and now able to take on any customer, anywhere.
Market	Direct sales complete to local clients in region 1.	Direct sales from region 1 staff into region 2.	Direct sales in region 2. First reseller agreement in region 1.	Licensing agreement to Tier 1 supplier. Four reseller agreements regions 1 & 2.
HR	$x # employees	$x # employees Labor costs are contingent upon software implementations and management contracts.	$x x ## employees Labor costs spike as new location is established in region 2. Recruitment of CEO & CTO.	$xxx #### employees Labor costs spike as new location is established in region 3.
Product Marketing	Marketing the Company is a continual outbound sales effort. Resellers are ineffective at this point. Technical people normally required to assist in sales process.	Direct sales still exclusive market route. Case studies and third party test results begin to reduce length of selling cycle.	As market begins to contact the company for orders, resellers and distributors begin to produce limited volume, but at a high cost as channel management team is constructed.	Market opportunities create need to expand product line. Competition heating as other products improve and product margins decline.
Alliance Targets	0 Mid-tier	1 Mid-tier	2 Mid-tier, 1 Major	6 Mid-tier, 3 Major
Finance	Founders Capital $	Founders, Family & Friends $	Venture Capital $	Banks $
Development	Prototype Development & launch	Version 2 release & continued innovation	New Product to begin product family or platform development	Acquisition of assistive technologies, continued innovation

What's a Due Diligence Binder?

Unless you're a General Partner of a venture capital firm, you're often tasked with filtering through the flurry of incoming business plans, phone calls and meetings that will hopefully find you that one deal, which the firm will fund and ultimately derive a successful exit. Deals referred to you by people you trust are certainly more interesting than deals that come over the transom cold. But let's assume that you are like most entrepreneurs and don't have a direct connection to the VC. Many times I've heard entrepreneurs lament about the length of time that was taken by the VC to complete the due diligence period. "He asked for some information, we sent it. Then he asked for more, we sent it. Then he asked for some stuff that we didn't have ready, so we had to build that and send it." And on and on. The lesson here is that you should have your due diligence binder ready before you pitch them.

Let's say the VC read your plan and gave you a call. Imagine his surprise when instead of answering his first question, you ask him the following: "Would you like for me to just send you the due diligence package? We've just completed it so that we could begin approaching VCs." I guarantee you right now that he will be very impressed. In addition to the materials listed in Chapter 8, basic due diligence requirements are listed but are not limited to the following:

1. Resumes and references of management

2. Resumes of advisors and/or board members

3. Patent information

4. Incorporation documents

5.   Share price history

6.   Share structure history

7.   Capitalization table history

8.   Financial statements (some may ask for these since inception)

9.   Employment agreements

10.   Management contracts

11.   Sale agreements

12.   Client contracts

13.   Client contacts

14.   Lease agreement(s)

15.   Debt agreements

16.   Agreements with market partners

17.   Minute book

There will be more information that they will ask for, however, you have significantly increased your level of professionalism if you can provide this immediately when required.

9 FINDING INVESTORS
Nearby & Neighborly

It's still not yet the right time to hit the market. Before you begin, consult your securities lawyer. The lawyer will need to review your materials to determine that you are on side with securities law. Your lawyer will also explain what you can and can't do when raising capital. Listen to the advice. Trouble with the securities regulators won't help your fundraising efforts or your reputation. Where you begin is largely dependent upon where your company is in its growth cycle.

The Love Money

Mom and Dad, Uncle Frank, the neighbor, your friends, and your old boss. These people write checks for young companies every day in North America. After the budding entrepreneurs run out of cash, they often tap into Love Money, the financial backing of friends, family and business associates. Treat them as professionally as any investor. Go through the process of the call, the meeting, and the presentation. It's good practice. If they invest, it's likely because they like and trust you. Sometimes will they will also invest because they like what you're doing. There will be some support from this group and if you continue to treat them professionally and keep them up to date with your progress, you may be able to access additional and more significant capital later. However, I would be remiss in not including a note of caution here. People get very strange where money is involved, even when it goes well. An Alberta entrepreneur built a very successful company over a five year period. When it came time to raise growth capital in Year 2, he opened up the offering to his family and friends. When a larger company came along and bought the company out in Year 5, the entrepreneur readied himself for a lot of good times and relaxation. Instead, he faced anger and resentment. Most of them were happy with the buyout, however, several were angry that the company sold when they did. They felt that if they had kept building the company, the buyout would have been even bigger. Others were mad that the entrepreneur got a big payday and they only made an annual rate of return over twenty percent. Jealousy is a sick, ugly beast and when it devours family and friends, it can sour and even destroy relationships.

Venture Capital

Not every company is suitable for venture capital even if it is a great company. Sectoral influences, timelines to exit, growth rates and a host of other factors can eliminate your deal from venture capital applicability. Venture capital is a major growth catalyst for many companies, but only a small percentage of the overall source of capital. Accessing venture capital is not easy, but if you have the right mix of team, product, opportunity and planning, it is available and it wants to meet you. But keep abreast of the money market trends. Historically, venture capital has been a distant second to angel and other private funding sources. Venture capital can be worth the effort, if you make sure you fit the criteria of what they seek. Find the venture capitalist that provides more than just capital and, most importantly, ensure that your end goals are in alignment.

But we were turned down by twenty venture capital firms

Make very certain that you are pursuing relevant capital. This should be obvious, but it happens all the time. Make sure that you match the criteria of the venture capitalists you contact. If they prefer consumer markets and you're a network security firm, you're wasting everyone's time. Also make sure that you match their preferred growth stage, and financing amount. The one requirement that is up for negotiation is location. They may state that they need you to be within sixty minutes of their office, however, this area of the "rules" has been bent more often than any other. It used to be the venture capitalists wanted their firms within a sixty minute drive, and then it changed to a sixty minute flight. Now distance is still a consideration, however, they just want a great company and it is much less of a top tier concern than it used to be if they can syndicate the deal with a trusted venture partner that is local to the deal.

Now here comes the tough answer. If you matched all of the requirements of the dozens of venture capitalists you pursued and were still unsuccessful, you may have to make the admission that you're not ready yet and that you must go back and make everything better. But first find out what needs to improve.

After the rejection, ask the venture capitalist for some specific feedback, but be very careful how you do this. As it often leads to an uncomfortable conversation, they likely will not want to give feedback. Instead you'll hear things like, "We're allocating funds to other areas right now" or "This is interesting, but just not what we're looking for right now". These are generic blow-offs reminiscent of the "It's not you, it's me" line you might have heard in high school or college. If they give honest feedback to you, thank them. Even if you don't agree with the feedback, thank them and leave. They've made up their minds and arguing with them now will not serve you well. If you're hearing the same feedback repeatedly, you likely have found the source of your problem whether you agree with it or not.

Typical Rejection Lines

The venture capitalist that sees hundreds of deals per year has to say no to almost every single deal. Typically, they invest in 1 out of 100 deals. Rejecting deals is difficult for most people, so they create ways to turn away deals and still leave the entrepreneur feeling good. It's called the Elegant Turndown. Some lines sound like this:

- "When you reach level X, we'll take another look."
- "If you find a lead investor, call me again."
- "We're currently over-weighted in your sector."
- "Call me in six months if you achieve X."
- "I'll put you on our watch list. So let's get back in touch next year."

These turn downs contain no criticism of the company pitching a deal. The entrepreneur leaves and doesn't feel the same sting of rejection that accompanies a blunt "You're not ready." But keep in mind that if the venture capitalist had to go through the full explanation and argument with every approaching entrepreneur, they wouldn't get any work done. So the elegant turn down helps them to move along and get on with their day.

By the way, if you get mad and burst into flames, you have just demonstrated that you can't control yourself and no one wants to partner with that kind of emotional immaturity. Similarly, if you're sniping about being rejected by one investor to another…I hope you get my point. The venture capital community, within its sector and region, is fairly tight-knit. If you've made a fool of yourself by blowing up at the turn-down messenger and you require venture capital, you might consider closing up shop and getting a job because you're likely done. This holds true after the deal as well. If you're a die-hard entrepreneur you'll likely want to create several more companies. If you're successful with this one, the VC will likely run with you again if you're reasonable to work with.

But If I'm Successful with This One, I Won't Need A VC For My Next Venture

The thought here is that because this venture went well, the entrepreneur will have enough financial capacity to fuel the next one. Perhaps, however, what this entrepreneur does not realize is that a great VC firm has tremendous power in its network, deal sourcing, partnering, joint venturing, recruiting and exit planning. Your next venture will likely need a partner with great skills and networks just as much as the first. It takes a village.

Find companies that were funded in similar growth stages from your industry. Make a list of the venture capital firms that supported those financings. As with everything, a great network is helpful. But while it might be helpful in generating an initial meeting, it does not help with getting to yes. You will also need a good pitch.

Below you will find a listing of Angel investor groups and seed-stage funds, organized by region as compiled by the National Angel Capital Organization. Visit www.angelinvestor.ca for listing updates.

USA
California
12 Angels - Los Angeles, CA
Band of Angels - Menlo Park, CA
European American Angel Club - San Francisco, CA
Golden Gate Angels - San Francisco, CA
Imporium Angels - San Diego, CA
Life Science Angels - Menlo Park, CA
Pasadena Angels - Pasadena, CA
Sacramento Angels - Sacramento, CA
Sand Hill Angels LLC - Menlo Park, CA
Tech Coast Angels - LA, Orange County, San Diego, Santa Barbara, CA
The Angels' Forum LLC - Los Altos, CA

Mid-Atlantic
Active Angel Investors - Vienna, VA
BlueTree Allied Angels - Pittsburgh, PA
Jefferson Corner Group - Charlottesville, VA
Jumpstart New Jersey Angel Network - Mt Laurel, NJ
LORE Associates - Philadelphia, PA

Mid-Atlantic Angel Group Fund I ("MAG") - Philadelphia, PA
Minority Angel Investor Network - Philadelphia, PA
Robin Hood Ventures - Wayne, PA
Virginia Active Angel Network - Charlottesville, PA
Washington Dinner Club - Washington, DC

Mid-West

Akron ARCH Angels (Akron Regional Change Angels) - Akron, OH
Centennial Investors - Columbia, MO
Core Network - Toledo, OH
Cornerstone Angels - Northbrook, IL
DePaul Blue Angel Network - Chicago, IL
Grand Angels - Grand Rapids, MI
Great Lakes Angels - Bloomfield Hills, MI
i2e Enterprise Oklahoma Venture Fund - Tulsa, OK
Irish Angels - Notre Dame, IN
Main Street Venture Partners - Fort Wayne, IN
Marquette University Golden Angels Network - Milwaukee, IL
Mid-America Angels - Lenexa, KS
Midwest Venture Alliance - Wichita, KS
Nebraska Angel Network - Lincoln, NB
NEW Capital Fund - Appleton, WI
North Coast Angel Fund - Cleveland, OH
Ohio TechAngels - Columbus, OH
Origin Investment Group - La Crosse, WI
Phenomenelle Angels - Madison, WI
Queen City Angels - Cincinnati, OH
RAIN Source Capital - St. Paul, MN
Silicon Pastures - Milwaukee, IL
St. Louis Arch Angels - St. Louis, MO
Stateline Angels - Rockford, IL
Wisconsin Investment Partners - Madison, WI

National

Listing of US Angel groups - Angel Capital Association
Investors Circle - Brookline, MA
Irish Angels - Notre Dame, IN
The Wedgwood Circle - Burke, VA

New England

Angel Healthcare Investors LLC - Newton, MA
Angel Investor Forum - Old Saybrook, CT
Bay Angels (Boston) - Boston, MA
Beacon Angels - Boston, MA
Boston Harbour Angels - Boston, MA
Boynton Angels - Worcester, MA
Cherrystone Angel Group - Providence, RI
CommonAngels - Lexington, MA
eCoast Angels - Portsmouth, NH
Golden Seeds LLC - Stamford, CT and Boston, MA
Granite State Angels - Hanover, NH
HubAngels - Brookline, MA
Launchpad Venture Group - Wellesley, MA
Maine Angels – Maine
North Country Angels – Vermont
River Valley Investors - Springfield, MA
Walnut Venture Associates - Wellesley Hills, MA

New York

Dutchess County Angel Network - Poughkeepsie, NY
Golden Seeds - New York, NY
New York Angels - New York, NY
Orange County Angel Network - Goshen, NY
Rochester Angel Network - Rochester, NY
Tech Valley Angel Network - Albany, NY
Tristate Ventures, LLC - New York, NY

Northwest

Alliance of Angels - Seattle, WA
Bellingham Angel Group - Bellingham, WA
Boise Angel Alliance - Boise, ID
Portland Angel Network - Portland, OR
Tacoma Angel Network - Tacoma, WA
Women's Investment Network (Oregon) - Portland, OR
ZINO Society - Seattle, WA

Southeast

Ariel Savannah Angel Partners - Savannah, GA

Atlanta Technology Angels - Atlanta, GA
Blue Ridge Angel Investment Network (BRAIN) - Asheville, NC
Charleston Angel Partners - Charleston, SC
Emergent Growth Fund - Gainesville, NC
Fund for Arkansas' Future - Little Rock, AR
Huntsville Angel Network - Huntsville, AL
Inception Micro Angel Fund - Greensboro, NC
Misissippi Angel Network - Ridgeland, MS
Nashville Capital Network - Nashville, TN
New World Angels - Boca Raton, FL
Piedmont Angel Network - Greensboro, NC
Seraph Group - Atlanta, GA
Springboard Capital - Jacksonville, FL
Triangle Accredited Capital Forum - Wake Forest, NC
Wilmington Investor Network - Wilmington, NC
Winter Park Angels - Winter Park, FL

Southwest

Arizona Angels - Scottsdale, AZ
Camino Real Angels - El Paso, TX
Central Texas Angel Network - Austin, TX
Desert Angels - Tucson, AZ
Enterprise Oklahoma Venture Fund - Tulsa, OK
Houston Angel Network - Houston, TX
New Mexico Angels Inc - Albuquerque, NM
North Dallas Investment Group - Dallas, TX
The InvestIn Forum of Angel Investors - Dallas, TX

West

CTEK Angels - Denver, CO
Hawaii Angels - Honolulu, HI
Sierra Angels - Incline Village, NV
Transition Partners Limited - Boulder, CO
Vegas Valley Angels - Las Vegas, NV

CANADA

Alberta
Alberta Deal Generator – Edmonton & Calgary, AB
Venture Alberta - Edmonton & Calgary, AB

British Columbia
BC Angel Forum - Vancouver, BC
Fundamental Technologies II - Coquitlam, BC
Okanagan Angel Network - Kelowna, BC
VANTEC - Vancouver Angel Technology Network - Vancouver, BC

Manitoba
Winnipeg Angel Organization - Winnipeg, MB

Newfoundland
Newfoundland & Labrador Angel Network - Saint Johns, Nfld

Nova Scotia, New Brunswick, Prince Edward Island
First Angel Network - Halifax, NS

Ontario
Aprilis Ventures - Toronto, ON
Association for the Advancement of Safety Technologies - Hamilton, ON
Cleantech Angel Network - Toronto, ON
Georgian Angel Network - Collingwood, ON
Golden Horseshoe Angel Network - Oakville, ON
Golden Triangle Angelnet - Cambridge, ON
Infusion Angels - Waterloo, ON
ISCM - Innovation Synergy Centre in Markham - Markham, ON
Maple Leaf Angels - Toronto, ON
Northern Ontario Enterprise Gateway - Providence Bay, ON
Ottawa Angel Alliance - Ottawa, ON
Ottawa Capital Network - Ottawa, ON
Peterborough Region Angel Network - Peterborough, ON
Purple Angel - Ottawa, ON
Ryerson Angel Network - Toronto, ON

Southwestern Ontario Angel Group - London, ON
York Angel Investors - Vaughn, ON

Quebec
Reseau Anges Quebec - Montreal, QC

Saskatchewan
SAINT - Saskatchewan Angel Investor Network - Saskatoon, SK

Capital Source Databases and Other Resources
Alaska InvestNet - Anchorage, AK
Angel Capital Education Foundation - Kansas City, MO
AngelNet, the Indiana Angel Investment Network - Indianapolis, IN
European Business Angel Network - Brussels, Belgium
National Association of Seed & Venture Funds - Chicago, IL
Northern Ontario Enterprise Gateway - Providence Bay, ON
Pennsylvania Angel Network
Wisconsin Angel Network - Madison, WI

Sourcing Venture Capital

There are hundreds of venture capital firms in North America. While directories are available for purchase, a seemingly better option is to utilize an online directory which would allow you to parse the list of many down to a manageable and relevant few. There is no sense in approaching a venture capitalist that specializes in medical devices with your industrial coating opportunity. A web search of Venture Capital Directory will provide you many options.

USA Venture Capital

The National Venture Capital Association lists its more than 400 members at www.nvca.org. There is a fee to access the directory.

Canadian Venture Capital

The Canadian Venture Capital Association lists its members online at the following site: www.cvca.ca. The listing is alphabetical, but also can be found by category of interest.

It's Scotch O'clock and Tom's on Time

The restaurant was beautiful. Windows stretched from shining dark wood floors to meet a soaring vaulted ceiling that lowered sparkling lighting back down to chatty diners. The fireplace warmed those still damp from the rain and music smoothed over the clink of silverware on china. Tom surveyed the tables of Titan management, board members, employees and spouses. The mood was boisterous. Everything looked perfect. Louise looked over at Tom and took his hand in hers. She smiled at him. He met her gaze, nodded and almost smiled back.

Gripping his glass, he thought back to the phone call.

"Hey Tom, it's Peter from ABC Ventures. I've got some news for you, but I'd like to meet in person. Just the two of us, okay?"

Tom sat down to meet later that day at Peter's office. Peter got right to it.

"Okay. We've completed our due diligence and there are a lot of things that we are really excited about here. The customers love the product, you've got great margins, growth is reasonable and we think that with some added research and development money, further products could help expand the market and reduce the risk of being a one trick pony. "

"Great. So we'll close on the financing?"

"That's what I wanted to talk to you about. The more digging we did, the more we understood the resistance from customers that would otherwise use your product."

Tom's mind flashed to those many meetings where he and David would be scratching their heads as they drove away from meetings that they thought had gone well but ended in rejection.

"What is it?"

"You."

Tom laughed.

Me?

"Try not to take it personally Tom. They like what you're doing, they even like you. But you're selling to an industry dominated by guys that have been running their companies for a decade at a minimum and usually a lot longer than that. They want to buy from the same guys that they have always bought from. They're also more than a little nervous about dealing with a small company and the repercussions that it would have on their production lines if you couldn't deliver for a period. In short, it comes down to trust. It's not that we don't trust you, we do. But in this case, our trust doesn't matter. The customer has to trust Titan. One name kept coming up as we learned more about this sector. Hargrove Peterson. Seems like he's the godfather to these guys. They trust him. He built a company over a twenty five year period and helped a lot of these other guys along the way. I understand you've met with him. So here's what we want to do. Our offer of $5Million stands. But we want to make a management change."

"By management change, you mean me."

"Yes. These guys place a lot of trust in Hargrove. They'll buy from him and the company will grow a lot faster than it is now. And frankly, we like his experience."

"What happens to me?"

"Hargrove will come in as CEO. You'd step down."

"Down or out?"

"You would certainly still be valuable in another position in the company. We would prefer that to you leaving entirely, however, we've often found that founders don't stick around very long after giving up the leadership role."

"What if I don't want to step down?"

"We shake hands and go our separate ways."

"Meaning, you pull your offer?"

"Yes."

Tom snapped back to the evening's festivities and looked over towards Jim and David. Jim quickly looked away. David raised his glass and nodded. Tom had taken the offer back to all the partners, but he knew they had to take it. They didn't have enough cash to fund the growth on their own and things were getting far past tight. None of the partners had taken a pay check in several months and the business was still losing money. Tom saved them from having to offer their opinion. He simply stated that he would be leaving the company.

While the thought of leaving was difficult to process, Tom didn't entirely hate the idea. He had really enjoyed bringing a solution to a problem. The start phase was wildly exciting when everything was new. But after they grew, the role of leader turned into more managing that what he had envisioned. He had done a fair job of delegating the work and hadn't micro managed, but the constant follow-up that he had to do to make sure his people were getting things done was a constant irritant. There was just a lot more babysitting than he had imagined. But still, the thought of leaving his idea, his invention, his baby, was difficult to process.

After dinner, Peter gave a glowing speech about Tom and presented him with a Rolex to whistles and applause. Tom, as agreed, would talk about the great employees, the accomplishments of the past and then direct their attention to the future. He felt rather odd, disconnected in that same foggy feeling as wandering through an overseas airport at 2am where nothing seems to make much sense. *Hmmm. No signs are in English and no one here speaks my language. They all seem to know where they're headed, but I'm not so sure. Is that a monkey? Hey, that guy was on my flight. Maybe if I just follow him, I'll find my luggage. Why is my cheek sticky?* He then directed their attention to the future of Titan which now lay in the hands of Hargrove Peterson. They shook hands and Hargrove said a few words about the outstanding growth prospects for the company and how much he looked forward to getting to know everyone. It went well.

10 THE PITCH
How Not to Kill Your Deal in 9 Minutes

Technology has put the power of professional grade photographic equipment well within the reach of the consumer market. Has the technology enabled some consumers to produce professional quality work? Absolutely. Does this mean that all consumers that purchase this quality equipment are now professional photographers? Certainly not. Quality tools combined with sufficient knowledge, experience, and talent can produce a great photographer. The same can be said for presentations. Technology has put the power of professional grade presentation software and hardware well within the reach of the entrepreneurial marketplace. Without study of what makes a great presentation, they then create a presentation that they believe is better than anything the investor will have seen previously. I have met very few entrepreneurs who believe that they arc bad presenters or have created a bad presentation. But consider the entrepreneur. This person is likely a very confident individual and generally of the opinion that they can do almost anything. The result is a lot of really, really bad presentations that are also poorly delivered.

In a first look presentation, the investor(s) generally only want an overview. If you hit the high points across the all-important areas of the proper six-pitch (see below), they will then decide if they are willing to invest the time to learn more. So, if you are presenting to an investor for the first time, understand that the first presentation objective is only to convince your audience that this is an opportunity worthy of their time to investigate further. Generally, if you sufficiently capture the following elements of the proper six-pitch, you'll increase your chances of finding a potential investor willing to learn more about you and your company.

The Proper Six Point Pitch

1.   Your solution solves what problem?

2.   What is your market?

3.   How will you pursue this market?

4.   Who is on the management team?

5.   What is the intended use of proceeds?

6.   What is the offer?

Opening: Always start with a quick opening that tells the story. Every listener to every pitch is generally holding out for something. What do they do? How much to they need?

Example: "Hi. I'm Tom, CEO of Titan Coatings where we make a coating for our customers to extend the life of industrial parts. We are looking for $5Million to expand our operations to meet demand."

Two sentences and it tells the whole story. Brevity is beautiful.

In this example, the audience or listener is aware of what you do, financial needs and use of proceeds. You have just set the stage that signals that this entrepreneur might be the one.

1. Your solution solves what problem?

In the Tale of Tom, their chemical application to industrial parts allows the parts to extend their working life. In 90 seconds it doesn't matter how that occurs. In 90 seconds, it just does. The longer discussion can occur in the Q&A. The customer will want parts to last longer because a machine with downtime for parts replacement costs $xxx/hr. in lost revenue. The chemical application reduces downtime, lost revenue and related costs by XX%, creating a client ROI in XXX operating days.

That should be it. Everybody understands and can relate to operating costs. They could have gone into the myriad other applications. No. That would show that they were unfocused. That would also weaken the clarity of the market need/solution equation.

2. What is your market?

Talk clearly about the market you can reach now and, if different, the market you can reach should you successfully attract the necessary capital. If your new product replaces the traditional tongue depressor, your market is not the multi-billion dollar global life science supplies market. It's not the North American medical supplies market. Pare it down to the item and what you can reach. If your new product reduces purchase costs by half, then cut the number that currently exists! If your budget limits your company to regional travel then the tongue depressor marketplace is really your immediate concern and is relevant to the reachable territory.

3. How will you pursue this market?

If you are using a direct sales approach and are already selling product, have your metrics ready. How many calls must your company make to generate how many leads, which results in one sale? This scale will allow you to show reward vs. cost metrics that few other entrepreneurs have bothered to create. Then show your sales cycle process, which identifies how each prospect is managed through the sales cycle and how each client is managed after the sale is complete. Because you look so very prepared, the investor will be impressed.

If you are using a third-party reseller approach and are already selling product, have your metrics ready. The same scale requirement exists here, however, you will also need to show your reseller channel program. Signing resellers is not that hard, driving volume through a channel can be very hard. Show the program that will identify how your company houses a superior channel management structure and process. Typically, a reseller market only works once the market is pulling product through the channel and you are relying much less on your reseller channel to go out and push the product.

4.   Who is on the management team?

Very quickly and clearly identify which positions are critical to the success of the company. Then explain how each position has been filled by the appropriate individual or, if one of the spots remains open, identify the skill set of the individual that is about to join and fill the team slate. One of these will need to have previously built a company. Ideally, that would be the CEO. Have references ready for the whole team.

5.   What is the Offer?

Since "the ask" is what the whole presentation is about, don't forget to ask. You need money, they have money. Hopefully, you have created a financial opportunity that is so compelling that they are excited to hear the ask. You need to show a financial opportunity that is unmatched. If they can make more money somewhere else than by investing in your company, the sophisticated investor should and will do just that. Make sure the investment opportunity is a winner for you and for them too. Sophisticated angel investors seek returns that mirror that of the upper quartile venture capitalists that pursue annualized returns over 25%.

If you're learning this for the first time, be aware that private equity investing in emerging companies is tough game. Most angel investors will not make money. Target returns like these are necessary. The sophisticate investor undertakes significant due diligence prior to investing. Some of the companies will die, some of them will always seem like they are about to take off, but never be able to soar very high. Hopefully, one or two will rise beyond common performance and make it big. The big return is necessary for the enormous risk that accompanies angel investing.

6.   What is the intended use of proceeds?

You can state in summarized terms how the money will be used, however be prepared to show the cash flow statement, which illustrates exactly what is happening to the money once the investment is made.

Slides

If you feel that you want to use an electronic presentation, fine. Keep the slide deck to 12 slides maximum. 12 is a lot, so you'll have to be very quick. At 90 seconds per presentation element, you're switching slides every 45 seconds and diverting attention away from the presenter 12 times during the 9 minute presentation. That is getting very close to too much switching. I like to keep it fewer than 10. Investors participate with entrepreneurs that they like and trust. If your slides keep attention away from the presenter, how will the investor get to know the entrepreneur?

Take a look at your slides. Make sure you can absorb the message within 5 seconds of first looking. The slide changes, the investor glances at it, then refocuses attention back to you. The slide should not say what you are saying. If your speech is identical to the text of the slide, why are we presenting redundant information? The slide should contain either brief bullets that simply refer to what you are elaborating upon or the slide should contain a support reference of text or illustration to backup what you are presenting verbally.

The 9 Minute Marvel

Complete the proper six point pitch in 9 minutes. Getting the message across in that first formal presentation with a prospective investor should be done in a concise manner. This allows 90 seconds for each one of the six elements of the six-pitch.

But I can't possibly describe my solution in 90 seconds!

Then you are not ready. You should be able to communicate what it is that you do in less than 10 seconds. Remember, at this first presentation, you are only attempting to convince your audience that they need to investigate the opportunity further. There will be ample time later for a lengthy product discussion.

That may be true for others, but my technology is highly complex and requires significant explanation for the audience to understand a) the magnitude of the opportunity [or] b) the genius of the technology.

Then you have no idea how truly far from ready you are. If you put forward a decent presentation, you will get every opportunity to describe everything in full detail.

I have prepared many entrepreneurs for investor presentations and, in my opinion, there are a few absolutes. Be clear in your opportunity, but get to the Q&A as fast as you can. As hard as it is, you want the investors talking and asking questions. Taking more than 9 minutes is never, ever better. It is very common for entrepreneurs to think that more is better than less, and that continuing to heap the great aspects of their business onto the listening audience is the key to becoming interesting. I cannot stress this enough. Wrap things up at 9 minutes, then get into the questions and answers, which is more important than you can imagine. A good presentation only sets the stage for a great Q&A session.

For those of you who get it, skip this paragraph. If you need some reasoning as to why 9 minutes is important, read on. I have seen and given many investor presentations and prepared many other entrepreneurs to present their opportunities. As coach to these companies, I normally sit near the front on the side with my chair somewhat askew so that I am able to watch the entrepreneur and audience. Some of the most exciting pitches begin to lose their luster after 9 minutes. Pass the 10 minute mark and you'll start to lose people. Pass the 12 minute mark and, in some cases, you can practically smell the death of the deal. You can see it in the facial expressions of those in the audience and in their body language. Prospective investors are generally successful people with little time to spare. So by the 9 minute mark, they have made their decision whether or not they want more information or not. If they do, then they will take part in the Q&A, if they don't, then they start to think about other things. They'll cross their arms, start shifting in their seats, stare blankly, look down, look up and look around. More importantly, there is no good reason to make something take longer than it needs to be and yes, all great presentations are under 10 minutes.

The Opening

Congratulations. You've earned an opportunity to present to people with money. As they are with every other significant meeting of your life, first impressions are important, so open well. This means you do not open with fumbling about. Engage your audience. 99% of all presenters do not bother or even think to engage the audience. A great presenter opens with a hook and a hanger. The hook is a question that is asked of the audience. They did not anticipate that they would be expected to participate. They've seen so many mundane and long presentations, they came with a preconception of what to expect, and you therefore have shocked them a little. They will sit up and listen.

I once coached an entrepreneur that had developed a testing technology for milk processors. We had the entrepreneur ask the audience who had milk that morning. Most audience members raised their hand. That was the hook, an experience to which nearly everyone in the room could relate. The entrepreneur then stated that there was good news and bad news. The good news is that milk processors test the milk and send the samples to outside labs for analysis. The bad news is that results typically are not returned to the processor until long after the milk has been consumed by the public. And that is the hangar, a one-two punch, which relates to the hook or experience. Here was an opening that enabled everyone to understand the pitch in less than 20 seconds. The good news, bad news illustration infers a less than ideal market situation and a further inference that this entrepreneur possesses a solution.

It also forces questions and required participation from the audience. You immediately wonder what they are testing for. What did I just consume that this company believes to be potentially harmful? Will I die? Kidding. In this instance, the pitch then moved to *we are ABC Co. that builds test equipment for milk processing. We seek $1M to expand our marketing effort.* In most instances the two sentences above is the right opening, however, this entrepreneur had an extra opportunity to engage the audience.

The Q&A

The Q&A is just as important as the presentation, likely more. Sometimes entrepreneurs will psyche themselves up for a dynamic presentation and then deflate the excitement in the room by either coasting through the Q&A or not having practiced the Q&A session. Keep up the enthusiasm and the professionalism.

Show that you're ready. It always shows well and that the entrepreneur has done his homework, when a question is asked and the entrepreneur can pull up a new slide to support the answer given. Answer the question clearly and make sure that they are satisfied with the answer. I've seen entrepreneurs answer a question, the investor gives a shrug and the entrepreneur asks for another question! That entrepreneur just buried himself, not only with that investor, but also with the other investors who saw it happen. Additionally, there are no stupid questions. Please don't smirk at a question you deem ridiculous. At most presentations, an investor will ask about valuation. Here is not the time to discuss valuation. What you say is this, "We have developed a valuation in co-operation with our board of advisors. There is significant work that went into the findings and I would be happy to discuss this privately. But I will say that it is a reasonable valuation that is well within industry and market norms for a company at our stage of growth."

Stop talking as soon as possible. This is huge. Many entrepreneurs will use a question as a launch pad into an extended pitch. Again, answer the question clearly and be concise as possible. At this stage, brevity is your friend.

Many times, the CEO will give the pitch, and then call up the rest of the management team to field the questions. In most cases, this is unnecessary. The team will often do this for a number of reasons. They may want to give some air-time to the rest of the team. Usually, the CEO wants the team there to field questions outside of his/her comfort zone. Usually for companies in these stages of growth, the questions should easily be handled by the CEO. If there is a particularly tough technical question, the CEO can easily identify the CTO in the audience and defer to him or her. There are many risks in bringing up the whole team to field the questions. The CEO has polished and perfected the pitch and presentation. The rest have not, therefore they are not conscious that they have their hands in their pockets, that they are looking around the room while one of their colleagues gives an answer, that they speak in a monotone voice, that they are going on too long, etc... If teams are used in Q&A, practice in front of a friendly audience. Practice how you're going to stand, how the questions will flow through the CEO to the designate, and the signal to wrap it up. Practice watching the speaker with interest and occasionally nod slightly in agreement as if it were done subconsciously.

Answer the question once. This is important when teams are involved. It is very, very tempting for most people, to at least once during the Q&A, add commentary to an answer already delivered. "Further to that" and "I'd like to add another angle here" are common errors. The team member does not intentionally do this to look stupid. They do this because they honestly believe that they are adding value to the Q&A process. The trouble is that when the team adds to an answer, the real message to the audience is the following: We are not in synch. We are not all on the same page. I'm more intelligent or can communicate more effectively than my fellow team member. We have not done our homework to the extent that we all know the mission, objective, strategy, tactics or whatever else is being asked on the floor. Worse still, this is another one of those red flags that identify the entrepreneur that isn't ready. The more people it takes to answer a question, the less you deserve to yet be pitching.

At nearly every presentation, at the start of the Q&A, the investors wake up a little. They straighten slightly, lean forward, drop the hand from the chin, etc... It is now their turn to speak. These are often Type A people. Perhaps in their mind, you've been speaking long enough, it is now time for them to peel back the cover on your deal and discover what is under the hood. The Q&A period can go as long as the investors want. At this point, you have handed control over to them and if they want to ask questions for twenty minutes, that's their call. If you are presenting to a group of several investors however, limit the Q&A to 30 minutes or less. Thank them for their time and let them know that if there are more questions, you would be happy to answer them one on one.

The 9 minute presentation obviously leaves room for more "show" in the Q&A portion of the meeting. But now that you are into more of a "conversation" mode with the investor, try to introduce a new medium. Moving the Q&A to the whiteboard provides a new landscape to view and some interesting strength to your meeting. You'll want to keep the attention on you, so answering questions verbally is always good. You will however be well advised to whiteboard the key elements you wish them to remember. Rough sketches are always good too. They don't know what you're drawing. You are revealing something to them in front of their eyes as if you are all discovering it together. Lastly, you're in action. They've already heard you speak, scrutinized your manner, and judged your clothing and slides. Now they've seen you illustrate on the fly.

Sure-Fire Statements to Sink Your Deal

"I'm a big picture person" or "We can hire folks to worry about the details"

These are beauties. This entrepreneur believes that his idea is so compelling, so worthy of awe, we needn't be so small-minded as to ask questions. This person is also under the false impression that a business idea, in and of itself, has value. What this entrepreneur does not understand is that this statement is interpreted as code for either, "I'm much too lazy to do the necessary work" or "I have no idea how to do this". This entrepreneur is also exposing his inexperience. If they were experienced, they would already know that, for most businesses, both opportunity and death await in the details. Successful business people that label themselves as big picture people are also always concerned with proper planning.

They didn't get it

As much as it pains me to admit, I once uttered this very ridiculous statement. We had the investor in our boardroom. We gave our standard pitch that we felt was pretty good and he didn't seem to get enthused as most others did when they saw our opportunity. He left the building and we remained in the boardroom wondering what we did wrong. I lifted my head and stated to the others, "He didn't get it". My partners agreed with that sentiment and we all then went about our day feeling much better about what happened because with one sentence, I had convinced the team that the investor was the problem at this particular meeting. Yikes. This happens a lot. The pitch is done and the investor is less than thrilled. Maybe he didn't ask many questions or was just rather indifferent to the whole thing. This entrepreneur often leaves an unsuccessful pitch meeting with the self-serving thought that the investor could not comprehend the opportunity.

There are three possibilities at work here:

1.   The entrepreneur did not effectively communicate the opportunity.

2.   The deal stinks.

3.   The investor simply found that this opportunity was not a match for his/her criteria. Criteria refers to the sweet spot where this firm prefers to participate, though it often means the deals they seek need to be good versus not good. Don't make the mistake that just because the investor chose not to invest that there is automatically something wrong with your deal. Many times, they are looking for something or someone else and no amount of further pitching will change that. Ask for their feedback, if they have something intelligent to say, learn. Do not argue with them. It's their opinion. Thank them for their time and contribution. Then let them go.

We have no competitors

Maybe because there is no market. Every product has an alternative, including status quo. Being a quantum factor better or faster or cheaper, does not eliminate competition. You may have a competitive advantage for this moment, however, market supply has never failed to respond to market demand.

If you happen to find yourself alone in a lucrative market, be very concerned, because competitors will be invading your space with a ferocity that exceeds the appetite of market adoption. Assume somebody somewhere is building something better than what you have and that they have more resources than you. This kind of paranoia will make you better and perhaps even stay alive in the market. Additionally, it will also prompt you to examine your market with a "what if" scenario. What if the bigger better came out of left field? Could your company survive as number 2? Is the market big enough for several market participants? If their product is cheaper, will a sufficient portion of the market stay with us because ours is better? You get the idea. Just remember that there will always be someone waiting to capitalize on an opportunity that you have uncovered.

Everyone else is years behind

This is seemingly similar to the We Have No Competitor lunacy previously discussed, however, upon closer inspection, we find that there is a separate and lurking danger to this common and seemingly harmless illusion. Many entrepreneurs believe that because they invested three years and $2Million to research and develop the technology, it will take others just as long or longer to do the same. Wrong. Your emerging competitor will see your technology in use at your client's facility. They'll be up to speed as to how it works and what you're doing in no time at all. What took you three years to figure out, is often learned by your nosy competitor in a matter of months or even weeks. If a patent blocks them, the risk is that perhaps they will look to find a work around. If you keep it a trade secret, they might be able to recreate what you've developed. Protect yourself as much as possible, then go as fast as you can. But don't ever think that you have the luxury of time with respect to competition.

Many entrepreneurs believe that no competitor could come up with the required mix of experience and skill sets that it took to build the solution.

The hard work is done

Brutal. It's fairly hard evidence of founderitis and carries the stench of deal going bad. This one is usually spewed by the research and development individual or crew that just surpassed the proof of concept. Somewhere, there must be a University (perhaps every University) teaching throngs of engineers or scientists that innovation is hard and business is easy. This statement, however, is never uttered by an engineer or scientist that has been down the track previously.

After my eighth divorce

The entrepreneur that has had repetitive nasty break-ups with a long string of other business partners is likely to continue the practice. The entrepreneur that can't keep it together and has repeatedly demonstrated this incapacity is branded appropriately and best left aside.

The technology is spectacular

The red flag on a statement like this is that the entrepreneur doesn't understand that it just doesn't matter. It may even be a bad sign. New technology is often referred to as cutting edge or bleeding edge. It cuts and bleeds because the ratio of lost dollars increases exponentially the closer you get to that edge. Innovation is terrific. However, a skilled, sophisticated investor will pursue the opportunity that will provide a target return that is reflective of their appetite for risk.

Maybe it is an acquired taste, but there is real beauty in business simplicity. Spectacular technology has its place, however, a lot of entrepreneurs might do themselves a favor by keeping their solution as simple as possible.

My company is worth fifty million dollars today

We are often met with inventors who over-value their company at this, as of yet, precarious stage. Too many inventors and entrepreneurs seek investment but are not prepared to offer reasonable equity participation to the investment community in exchange for the necessary growth capital. Inevitably they end up months and years later without progress, deeper in personal debt, still clinging to an idea that they must maintain ownership of all or nearly all of the company.

The other thing that happens is that the entrepreneur finds unsophisticated investors that support the inflated value by investing at the price desired by the entrepreneur. Because the offering was filled, the entrepreneur feels justified in his valuation. Inevitably, the delayed boom is lowered. The second or later round of financing finds professional investors who won't accept the valuation. So in order to attract further capital, the entrepreneur has to roll back the value of the company to a more realistic level. The result is that the founders and first round investors then get hit hard because their ownership stake is now dramatically reduced. It is very common that first round investors get crammed down because the entrepreneur sold round one at too high a value. The other option is that the entrepreneur attempts to sell the company to reach an exit only to find that buyers need upside too. You have to leave some opportunity for the next owner of this company. Because the entrepreneur over-valued the company initially, the buyout value is a disappointment for everybody.

Our technology is applicable to six vertical markets

Again the weakness of inexperience rears its ugly head and I can include myself in this criticism. I once thought I could take on several technologies and sell them into their respective, but unrelated, markets. The truth, as I found out, was that time, personnel and the lack of financial resources were such limiting factors, we simply could not do it all. We learned that lesson in the span of a few months, put all of our time and resources behind the product that was gaining traction and shut down every unrelated effort. Likewise, you will most likely have to choose your best opportunity and pursue it harder than you ever thought you might have to.

Disclosure, Ethics & Common Sense

Imagine finally finding an investor that is willing to take the risk with you. Imagine having gone through the months of due diligence. Then imagine the teams from both sides getting to the lawyer's boardroom where champagne sits waiting in the corner as the reams of documentation is signed. The venture capitalist notices something on one of the sets of documentation that he needs to sign, checks it against a copy in his briefcase, and tears up the check. The entrepreneur goes ballistic.

What the venture capitalist noticed is that the entrepreneur tried to slip in a fairly significant bonus for himself. He tried to do it without mentioning it and therefore wasn't treating the new financier as a partner. With one greedy, underhanded, loser move, the trust was gone and so was the funding. The odd thing is that this happens all the time. Maybe not in the same way, but many venture capitalists have stories of entrepreneurs that have outright lied or otherwise tried to hide commitments, debts, information and a lot of other elements that need to be shared. Venture capitalists understand that not everything is perfect. No company ever is perfect. They will appreciate your honesty and your maturity to admit that something isn't quite right. Don't be a schmuck. Treat the investors the same way you would wish to be treated if you were the investor, and you'll do yourself a lot of favors.

I'll Never Give up Controlling Interest

I once met with a management team with a transportation business that was taking off in a way that was allowing the team to consistently surpass sales and profitability targets. Major clients called them for business. The team had purchased a technology from a one-time supplier and had ended up owning the technology and related patents after the supplier company went out of business. The transport company continued to better the technology and after shifting target markets, found that there was tremendous value in the related opportunity. But because the core business had become a proven money-maker, the team neglected the up-and-comer product and as a result, the homerun technology was choked of human and financial resources. An outside, but experienced management team approached the transport company to spin-out the technology into a new company. The new team would invest several million dollars and run with the new technology into the marketplace. The first team could not accept the idea that someone else would run with their product, nor could they accept that they would, at the end of the second tranche of funding, own less than 50% of the spinout. Predictably, the team did not agree to the deal and the opportunity never went anywhere. They maintained their 100% ownership of zero. Congrats. Well done.

In short, put yourself in the shoes of your prospective audience. You too would want a clear, concise message delivered by a polite professional person who was ready.

11 ABOUT INVESTORS
Sorting Through the Groomed and the Guilty

Normally, when I'm asked to give a talk about how to raise capital, I present a fairly nuts and bolts overview, of what is required for capital attraction. However, often overlooked are the reasons behind why sometimes the seemingly obvious deal goes un-funded.

Tom has a company and it has been determined that the company will require capital to grow. Tom and his team have worked very hard to get the company in motion. The products were built quite well and customers seem to like them. There seemed to be a decent market and the whole deal looked quite exciting. Yet, even though investors appeared impressed by the deal, a very low percentage of investors that are pitched actually invest. A large population of entrepreneurs are confused by this pattern of behavior. Why does this occur? The answer is quite simple. The entrepreneur has not yet recognized that the investor is a prospective customer.

Entrepreneurs need to change the view they currently hold of an investor to match the view they currently hold for their customer. Most teams, by and large, will go to incredible lengths to win their first customers. Countless hours are poured into product research, design, development, testing, focus groups, redesign, redevelopment and re-testing. They interview prospective customers to learn about them. They learn what they like, what they hate. What is really important and what is just window dressing. They go to these great lengths so that they can return with a great product, a technology so compelling, that there is no way they can turn us down. This product is so great, they will be unable to stop themselves from giving us their money, so that they might get the opportunity to incorporate this technology into their company. This technology embarrasses all other competing products. The investment opportunity in your company is your product that you must sell. Make sure it is just as compelling and just as well suited to this prospective investor who is really another customer. Make sure you are so well prepared that investors can't wait to give you their money.

Make sure you are so well covered off on the important elements that you embarrass other companies seeking money, because these are your competitors for that investment dollar.

Give the investor, your customer, what they want. What many of them want is:

- Ready Product – few investors will be eager to pay for prototypes, that is usually the responsibility of the founders, their family and friends. This won't be possible in some cases, but try. It's much easier for an investor to get into a deal when customers are using the product.

- Near Term Profits – early profits reduce risk and can point to an early exit

- Sustainable Market Advantage – if you spend a lot of effort only to prove out the market and your advantage is weak, competitors will show up in droves

- Potential for 10X Returns – otherwise why should they care?

- Management with previous wins - investors do not want you to learn on their dollar

- Early Exit – if your plan is to build and sell in ten years, most investors will seek another deal. A 3 year exit is quick. 8 years is long. Make a plan that stays in a normal range of 4 -7 years.

- Client IR – What does your product do for your customer? Does it make them money or save them money? If neither, it might not be a "must have" product and it might be a "nice to have" product. The product should be easily recognized to pay for itself in an impressive timeline for the customer.

Imagine you are selling your car privately. You seek someone with the money who will acquire your asset. You dress your asset as best you can to achieve the sale. You wash it, vacuum it out and hang a pine-scented piece of cardboard from the rear view mirror. The car looks good, drives well and has a lot of the options the buyer wants. But, there is a problem. It turns out your car has rust. You can't see it just by standing nearby. The potential buyer peeled back the carpet in the trunk and there it is. The potential buyer says, fix the rust and I'll buy the car. Your business is not different from this used car. It turns out your business needs a more experienced management team. The investor says, fix the team and I'll buy a piece of your company. The entrepreneur says, buy my car and I'll fix the rust at a later date. Who would buy that car? Nobody. And yet, that is what happens every day.

The entrepreneur says, give me the money and I'll get a team, a patent, an office, a customer, a product, a service, an affiliate, a reseller, an employee...Listen, you have something to sell. You are selling an investment. The investors are your target market. Devise a business plan to approach the investment community. Not every being on the planet is a target prospect for your product. Likewise, not every investor is a target for your company. Be the compelling star that shakes money from stone when you do find the right audience.

Market Shifts

Let's get down from the 10,000 ft. view and discuss the investment market for early stage companies. Angels have tired of taking a beating. Angel returns are generally poor, but they still want to invest. Actually, they still invest more than ~5X that of the venture capital participants. As a result of the mounting losses, they have sought education. They turn to investor networks and conferences to learn the investments skills of those better skilled. It is now not uncommon to see angels investing on the same term sheet as a VC. Now let's get from our market to the boardroom table where you find yourselves sitting across from the money.

Show Me the Money

Investors want what everybody wants. If you had $1MM to invest, what would you want? You'd want to buy the perfect deal, with all the right elements in place so that $1MM might become $10MM in a four to six year exit. We have previously believed that angels invest in areas of their comfort, but this is changing as they become better educated in the intricacies of angel investing. Like poker players, there are many who consider themselves experienced, but few are truly skilled. They want a great team to provide a great return with a logical exit in a reasonable timeframe. Still, you can have all these things and not get funded. When this happens, ask yourself this question. "Is my investment opportunity, the best opportunity available to this individual or this company?" If you do not believe that your opportunity is the best opportunity available, maybe you don't deserve the money.

Consider the pure investor. It is his job to maximize capital return. If they can make more money opening mini-malls, they should do that. If you don't truly believe in your heart that your company is going to drive return, it will show. It will show in your material, in your product and in your presentation.

The Unfunded

So the marketplace has changed, but the lot of first time entrepreneurs have not and it isn't surprising. How would you know if you haven't done it before? 90% of the business plans look exactly like this: a)unique product, b)big market, c)no competitors and d)3 years to fame and fortune. There is rust in the trunk, the brakes are shot and the oil has never been changed because this is a new driver who didn't know about auto maintenance.

Every business plan has projections. You should have them and I have no problem with these estimates but I do have a problem with projections that are not accompanied with detailed assumptions or highlighting certain essential elements. State your assumptions. Detail your plan. And show you know where all that fame and fortune is coming from and how.

12 ALIGNING INTERESTS
How Not to Kill Each Other

If you hang about the investment community, you'll hear a lot of discussion around alignment of interests. It really is very much like the couple that files for divorce once they have determined that they "want different things", "grew apart" or went Hollywood with "irreconcilable differences". Perhaps you know of people who went through just such a situation. What went wrong? They dated, had fun, enjoyed each other and got along quite well. And to look at them individually, they were very good looking, however together they were one of those magazine couples. Vacations worked out well and they even made it through one of the greatest tests of a marriage, a renovation of their home. Then one day, one of the partners determines that the road which this particular marriage is on is headed to a location that is determined to be favorable by one and highly unfavorable by the other. To their friends, it's a disaster. *"They were so good together"*. But perhaps the couple had never gone through the conversation of what life might look like in ten years ideally for each of them. Maybe one wanted to make just enough to retire early in a small rural community and live out their days taking their dog for walks and riding a bike. The other might have wanted to continue the upward course of their career, necessitating a move to increasing travel schedules and transfers to one urban center after another. Without a shared vision of what will be, the couple never had a chance from the start.

Entrepreneurs and investors need to have a similar conversation long prior to any issuance of a check or this marriage will too suffer the pains of separation. Perhaps the entrepreneur wants to build a large company and just keep building. And maybe, the investor wants the company to be sold within 5 years. At the outset, they got along; they were both excited by the opportunity, but never had that all-important conversation about the future.

But it's not just the down road picture that must be in sync. Objectives and related strategies will need to be agreed upon with the major investors. It's always easier dealing with fewer investors as compared to many. In this case, we are assuming that there are only a handful of investors that are backing the company. They need to be aware and on board with your plan, otherwise it's much too easy for them to blame you when life happens the way it often does.

Figure out today, what it is that you want and how everybody can get out when necessary. Then don't just talk about it, get a signed agreement that details how separation will be handled. Think of it as a pre-nuptial agreement.

In this chapter I would also like to talk a little about what to watch out for when pitching for money. Not every investor is right for you or your deal. As you come close to a deal with a prospective investor, make sure you complete your due diligence on the investor.

Very important: Not every dollar is equivalent.

But first, a note about common courtesy and behavior. Treat an investor the way you would like to be treated. The quickest way to lose the interest of an investor is to treat them like a checkbook. Most entrepreneurs have no idea that they are doing it, but they're blatant in their actions and self-defeating as result. Many entrepreneurs are friendlier to the prospective investor than they would be to anyone. That is, until they deliver the final answer of No. Then suddenly, the investor is dumb as a sack of hammers and is theretofore referred to in further disparaging terms. Word of this kind of behavior will find its way to either the first prospective investor that declined the deal or to the next prospective investor. In both cases, you've sunk your own ship. Perhaps the first investor would like to watch the company grow for a while before investing, but now that he heard of the criticism, the check won't be forthcoming. The next investor will recognize the disrespect for others and if he is a sophisticated investor, he'll walk.

Entrepreneurs should treat investors politely and respectfully. Entrepreneurs, however, should expect the same treatment in return, which brings me to the topic of this chapter.

Angel investors are simply people that have done well for themselves in one capacity or another. Perhaps they built a successful company or inherited a family fortune. Either way, they have the funds an emerging company usually needs to fuel the growth of NewCo.

In an ideal scenario, your deal has attracted such interest that you have the luxury of choosing your investor. Most entrepreneurs will take the first investment dollar that is offered. This I understand. Raising money for emerging companies can be incredibly difficult, so when money is offered, turning it away is not usually anybody's first reaction. The point here is to direct your search in such a manner that when cash is offered, it is likely then to be from an intended source. Examine your company and skills sets within. Perhaps Tom would have found an easier time of raising capital from people who have been successful in the same sector. Not only would that person be able to fund or partially fund the company, but that person might be an incredible wealth of information and assistance. So now Tom pursues Alfred who built a relevant company. Alfred is so enamored with the deal he agrees to fund the company. Additionally, he signs on as an advisory board member.

Alfred is retired, so he helps out a few hours every now and then. He introduces the company to good distributors and warns them away from the bad ones. He knows where better framing material can be sourced and how to build a more efficient assembly line. Alfred later brings in Jim, a CFO from his old company. Jim helps to improve the movement and efficiency of cash in the company. Later he finds one company to provide inventory financing for the organization and another that will do a sale and lease back of their equipment. As a result, the company is now not requiring another round of capital.

Alfred's money was less than 1/3 of the overall impact of Alfred's knowledge, experience and network. Strategic, smart and helpful money is worth far more than passive investment.

Ask the investor about previous deals in which they have been. Ask about the successes and the failures. Take note of how the investor reacted to situations when things weren't going well in a deal. Did he become a sideline critic or did they roll up the shirtsleeves and help out? Building a company is one of the riskiest ventures on earth, so try to make sure you surround yourself with positive, experienced, helpful people. Ask for references from other entrepreneurs with whom they have invested. If they have not invested previously, ask for references just as you would if you were considering hiring them for a role in the company. You spend more time at work than you will with your spouse, so choose all people carefully.

About the Bad Ones

Yes, bad investors are out there. I'm sure you are not shocked.

Here's a few warning signals:

Timmy Two-Face: This individual starts off by posing as an investor. They then morph into, "I'll consider investing, if you hire me to complete this [fill in the blank] for you." This "investor" will likely never invest a nickel. The most you will get is work in trade for stock in the company. He is essentially a consultant seeking gigs from entrepreneurs. Worse still, they are usually poor quality consultants. Consultants of quality have no reason to veil their trade.

Time Burglar Trish: This individual can't say no. As a result, an endless request for information will ensue, followed by "Let's wait until [X] happens." After several rounds of requests and deliveries of information, simply ask the question straight out. *"If I provide this information and you find it to be satisfactory, will you invest in my company?"* A non-committal answer is your red flag. You cannot do this right at the start, however, as the investor needs time to get to know the deal, the business and the team.

Vulture Vic: A perennial favorite. This person will take you and your company. Often, offers are made with a massive array of punitive terms and conditions that will often end up with this investor in control of the company. A very good securities lawyer should help you avoid a bad situation here. A favorite trick of these guys is to propose a convertible debt instrument that comes with payments. These instruments are not bad in themselves, but when administered by those with evil intent they can be perilous. Payments are usually high enough to make sure the entrepreneur will not be able to keep up with them. Entrepreneurs sometimes accept these deals for three reasons i) no one else is offering them any cash, ii) they are so optimistic about the future of the company that they are sure they can make those payments, or iii) they just didn't know about this practice. Upon default, the company usually ends up in the hands of Vic.

Larry Litigious: Your due diligence should discover how much time this guy spends in court. A guy who likes to use lawyers as his mode of leverage is best left aside.

About the Good Ones

There are a lot of good ones. Most people are inherently good and if the entrepreneur and the investor have worked through various scenarios of success and hardship right at the start, they will have already worked through the various points of disaster that befall many other relationships. A well thought out shareholders agreement is the ruling body in this relationship.

A good investor likely has some use to you other than money. They have money because they did something right. You can learn something from this person. If you're lucky, they are familiar with your industry and can teach you something or open doors to the right people. Perhaps this investor has built a company before and knows how to keep you from making the same mistakes he made. The Mentor capital that came with that venture capital is often more valuable than the cash itself.

13 THE CONCLUSION OF TOM
Is it Ever Really Over?

Tom stuck it out for the entire six months of transition and leaving felt a lot better than he originally thought as he didn't particularly enjoy being an employee at the company he started. Hargrove, as predicted, took to the task very quickly, racked up sales very quickly and had trimmed costs in small ways across a variety of elements that added up to fair change. Tom and Louise took a long needed vacation and spent a lot of time just hanging out together. He played golf most mornings and for a while thought doing very little was fun. That lasted about 3 months. He did however, enjoy his new Porsche 911. Practical? Maybe not. But the severance package had been pretty good and there was something in that exhaust note that seemed to act as sufficient therapy.

Today's excuse for driving was to drive past the electrical substation for their area. The power had gone out again and a call to the power company informed him that a crew would have power back on by the end of the day. The guys on site were readily engaged in conversation. Turns out a lot of power outages are caused by birds that land on the components. They showed him the roasted crow.

"So a bird lands on this stuff and power is gone for the whole area?"

"Yeah. We've tried a few things to keep them from landing on this stuff, but it still happens a lot."

Tom stood frozen for a moment.

"What about a coating?"

"What do you mean? Maybe. I don't know. We just fix it when it breaks."

Tom thanked the guys, walked quickly back to his car, flipped open his phone and called his wife.

"Honey, I've got an idea."

14 SUBJECT MATTER EXPERTS

Shawn Abbott on Leadership

Where the typical person finds occasion to complain, an entrepreneur is that rare person who instead sees opportunity. There is a strange selflessness inherent in this ability to internalize the challenges of others as possibility for one's self.

Successful entrepreneurs draw together disparate resources to create novel goods and services, a process which is not just the largest, but arguably the only true organic source of new employment and economic prosperity.

The successful venture capitalist seeks individuals with this "X Factor", but what exactly is it? It is multiple things, but there is a core.

This core is frequently characterized as a highly detail-oriented attitude toward the product and service being delivered to customers. But the true entrepreneur needs a much broader view than this outward appearance; an innovator first, perfectionist second, and leader through to the end.

The innovator requires agility; an unimpassioned detachment to see past the obvious. An instinct to know when to stay the course, to love and nurture the business as an offspring but also when to instantly cut bait and pivot without remorse. True listening to customers means hearing body language, seeing pain, feeling opportunity. Intuition is not dismissed by those skilled in these arts as it is by an MBA spreadsheet monkey. The innovator has an innate ability to envision a future without being encumbered by over-concern for obstacles that -- while monumental -- can ultimately be overcome.

The perfectionist requires individualism to choose the road less traveled. An unknown path is unsafe. All the world, both inside and out, will shout that the bar is too high, pragmatists will abound claiming the product is "good enough". Only the entrepreneur with a compass grounded in world-class domain expertise can hope to build a truly disruptive company.

The leader requires a deal-making ability to bring it together than can almost never be delegated to someone else. None can inspire the followship of early adopting customers like the founding entrepreneur. These customers are not acting out of rational economics, but out of a desire to participate in change. This business development skill -- an ability to make stone soup -- is essential.

While entrepreneurs are by nature tenacious, they are often unwilling to sustain the discipline necessary to build out these ideas at a detail level, which is why successful company building is most frequently a team sport. Which is why, although the star merits the most attention in an investment decision, the supporting cast will absolutely make or break ultimate success.

We are all born with a spirit of optimistic entrepreneurism, a spirit can develop into skill under adversity, but becomes shrouded by safety and security. Fostering this spirit is the greatest challenge of our education system because entrepreneurs are encouraged, mentored, funded and celebrated. But they are not hired; they are the ones who do the hiring.

Shawn Abbott
Partner
iNovia Capital
www.inoviacapital.com

About Shawn Abbott, iNovia Capital

A partner with iNovia Capital, Shawn Abbott has a passion for building communications and Internet start-up companies. Shawn is presently an investor and board member at Tynt, CoolIT Systems, SiXtron, Peraso and Reflex Photonics. He has played entrepreneur, investor, technical and general management roles across fifteen technology start-ups in three continents over 20 years. His work pioneering internet security as CTO, then President, at Rainbow Technologies (NASDAQ:RNBO) saw the company grow ten-fold in profitability before being sold to SafeNet (NASDAQ:SFNT) for nearly a half billion dollars. In the late 1980s, he established and built the AND Group, which pioneered the CD-ROM locking used on several million discs. He is an accomplished public speaker, having presented at more than one hundred conferences on digital security and entrepreneurism, and taught software design courses internationally. He is past chair of the Banff Venture Forum and on the Venture Capital

Association of Alberta executive. He holds an early patent as one of the inventors of now popular USB keys. His publications include a chapter on hardware cryptography in the ICSA Guide to Cryptography. Shawn earned his Bachelor's of Science in physics at the University of Alberta and has done postgraduate study at the University of Calgary, Stanford, and UC Irvine. Shawn is also an active rotary wing pilot.

About iNovia Capital

We manage relatively small venture capital funds, so that means we make our money when entrepreneurs and our investors make money (not on massive fees). We are not afraid to lead deals or invest alone. We like to make relatively small investments in seed stage companies that require limited capital to reach value creating milestones. Once these milestones are reached, we have the capability to follow-on in later rounds and offer capital to scale businesses and accelerate their growth. We have an outstanding network of angels, strategic partners and venture firms that we can draw on as co-investors and advisors. In any case, we don't let our fund economics dictate terms of a round, but prefer to let the companies' capital requirements drive round size. Speaking of terms, we believe in standard terms like those used by the NVCA (and soon supported by the CVCA).

Bob de Wit on Foundertitis

"Founderitis is definitely the leading killer of new ventures. Hard to diagnose but relatively simple to cure, it's a tough affliction for any entrepreneur to admit to. This chapter has outlined many of the symptoms, but what should the pro-active entrepreneur do to show prospective investors that they "get it?" The first thing to do is to remember

that every entrepreneur wears a second hat: that of an investor. As a significant shareholder, every entrepreneur would agree that a successful venture requires only the best leadership and governance. To assure the latter, we look for ventures that have a strong board with a majority of independent board members who measure the activities of management against objective milestones provided by management and approved by the board. Second, we like to see entrepreneurs who have set up reverse-vesting provisions. What are these? Reverse vesting places restrictions on founder's shares whereby the shares do not fully vest to the founder until time passes and milestones are reached. Not only does this preserve the capital of the company for proper allocation to effective leadership, it also encourages the creation of realistic milestones by founder-managers. But above all, it sends a powerful signal to investors that the founder has provided the antidote to founderitis and reduced the "people risk" of their investment."

Bob de Wit
Director & CEO
GreenAngel Energy Corp
www.greenangelenergy.ca

About Bob de Wit, GreenAngel Energy Corp

Bob de Wit is a Vancouver based investor, mentor, director and consultant to growth-stage technology companies. He expresses his passion for entrepreneurship as Executive Director of New Ventures BC, Director of GreenAngel Energy Corp, and as an active member of the VANTEC angel network and the WUTIF angel fund. Annually, he mentors or reviews the best of the new technology ventures coming out of British Columbia each year. As a frequent speaker on entrepreneurship, Bob draws upon his executive experience in corporate development (M&A strategy and execution), corporate finance (raising equity capital) and competitive market intelligence to audiences ranging from entrepreneurial CEOs, angel investors to graduate students. Holding degrees in marketing (BBA) and economics (MA) from Simon Fraser University, Bob has built his fifteen year career around starting or nurturing technology start-ups. In addition to working for companies, he has consulted to Simon Fraser University, the University of British Columbia and the University of California at Los Angeles where he has worked with university faculty members to develop effective technology commercialization strategies.

About GreenAngel Energy Corp

GreenAngel Energy Corp. is a green energy technology company. Our focus is commercializing new technologies that produce renewable energy, improve energy efficiency, or use renewable energy resources such as water, wind and solar. We also seek companies that deploy or manage technologies and processes that reduce greenhouse gas (GHG) emissions. Our approach provides shareholders with the opportunity to invest in green energy companies at very early stages when valuations are low, with the objective of providing substantial financial gains. We are always seeking promising companies to invest in and work with.

A Q&A with Bill McKenzie

WB: Assuming due diligence processes have returned data that would make the prospective investment appear promising and you then turn to complete due diligence on the entrepreneurs and their key team members, what are you looking for? What are some of the highlights and warning flags?

BM: As you know, it is an unusual combination of leadership plus management strength, cohesion and experience that investors seek in making a judgment call on whether to back a team to implement a plan to build a successful and valuable business.

Highlights include:

- leading domain knowledge-a clear understanding of the customer, competition and channels, the pain/problem the company is proposing to solve, plus the sales and marketing process and required resources;

- high energy with persistence and resilience;

- being really smart and intellectually curious;

- demonstrated ability to focus on the critical few tasks and get things done;

- being good listener and effective communicator;

- an ability to tell a compelling story, in the context of attracting talent, winning early customers and raising capital;

- leadership, including the ability to motivate intense and co-operative effort for an extended period;

- willingness to hire people who are smarter and more experienced and better than the founder, without being threatened;

- demonstrated leadership generally means having achieved results in a prior general management role, ideally in the same or a similar market and at a similar stage of development to what is proposed in the business plan;

- ideally a team that has worked together in the past-as there will be a lot of stresses and strains in the multi-year process of building a business, and a demonstrated ability to work together increases the odds of success;

- skin on the table (a meaningful portion of one's net worth invested in the company).

Warning flags include:

- lack of humility/maturity (unless you are Steve Jobs!);

- lack of respect for your competitors;-or for your investor's money;

- a history of not building enduring relationships, or a personal situation that is not consistent with working and travelling 6 or 7 days a week for 10 years to achieve commercial success;

- issues in reputation or ethics;

- a team that hasn't worked together, or at the phase of development the company is presently at.

WB: Do you have advice for entrepreneurs with respect to how they interact with investors both current and prospective?

BM: Have a realistic view of valuation; realize that the only path to enduring tenure for the entrepreneur as the business leader is to be a fast learner and good listener, and to achieve success; recognize that you are also a shareholder, and it is a lot better to be a founder of a business that goes on to be a commercial success (which can then be the foundation of the entrepreneur getting financed in a subsequent initiative) than it is to get in the way of the commercial management and market understanding that are needed to drive your business to success-just like Tom!

WB: This chapter is entitled Alignment of Interests. The reference here is that any company will be better off with the interests of the entrepreneur to be in perfect alignment with the interests of the investor. What do you do to maximize this element to best effect?

BM: Founder's equity ownership should vests based on milestones achieved; an appropriate balance of ownership between the key members of the management team; a balanced board of directors (different backgrounds, strengths and perspectives; careful reference checking by the entrepreneur on the reputation and value-added contribution of investors, as well as by the investors on the management team; anti-dilution (ratchet) clause; tag and drag along provisions so that investors and management can exit together and deliver 100% ownership to a strategic buyer.

WB: When all goes right with an investment, relational issues are less common. When it isn't going as planned, the relationships between the entrepreneur and investor can breakdown. Could you provide some advice for those entrepreneurs that are experiencing this right now or provide some key points that could help our readers from encountering this dilemma?

BM: Be honest and forthright on concerns and issues; communication content and style; be very candid and upfront on succession and exit issues, as Swagger & Sweat emphasizes; share the bad news early, in order to build confidence and address issues on a timely basis; volunteer weaknesses in your personal history and the company history prior to them being uncovered during the diligence process, in order to build trust and place the weaknesses in context-for example, what did you learn from these outcomes and relationships?; selecting legal counsel and other advisors who know how to get a deal done, and have done private financings in the past-so they can advise you effectively and focus on the important issues

WB: Any other element of the investor/investee relationship that ought to be touched upon?

BM: If you don't respect and like your partner, then your ability to work together will be compromised, which will get in the way of success. In assessing a source of funding, you should make reference calls to see how they deliver vs. their promises. The life-cycle stage of the fund in which an investment would be made can also have an important impact on the likelihood of your investors participating in subsequent rounds of financing-which is very important to successful fund-raising; do not under-finance your company-an extra $1 million in your current financing could give you necessary time to achieve important milestones, prior to seeking to raise additional financing.

About Bill McKenzie, Next Equities

Bill is Senior Advisor to Next Equities and a Director on its Advisory Board. He gained extensive experience in private investments plus corporate development by leading over 20 investments, and serving as a director of over 20 companies. Bill was Senior Vice President of Alberta Investment Management Corporation(AIMCo), where he led a team to source, assess, negotiate and actively manage international investments in excess of $2 billion. For 15 years, he was Vice President of Vencap, one of Canada's largest and most active private equity investors, assessing hundreds of investments and assisting portfolio companies on strategy, corporate finance and executive recruitment. Bill initiated investments that led to 5 companies being acquired by strategic buyers, 3 IPOs and 3 acquisitions of Vencap ownership positions. As Vice President Corporate Development of The Churchill Corporation (TSE), Bill led initiatives to accelerate growth, profitability and value. Bill holds a MBA from Harvard Business School and a B.B.A. from the University of Regina, plus designations as a Chartered Financial Analyst, Certified Management Accountant and ICD.D, the professional director program offered through the Rotman School of Business, University of Toronto. Bill is currently a director of several private companies.

About Next Equities

Next Equities targets promising western Canadian companies that are looking for private equity funding and complementary expertise to accelerate growth and profitability. Created to leverage capital, corporate relationships, and knowledge acquired by the Next Equities team as founders and operating executives in other ventures, we seek to be the established entrepreneur's first choice as a value-added partner. Next Equities looks to work with management in companies that have achieved market validation and have significant growth and value creation potential.

Next Equities is willing to consider minority and majority growth-capital opportunities, plus acquisitions, in a wide range of sectors. With our complementary management expertise in manufacturing, finance, sales and marketing, logistics, and international expansion, the Next Equities team will bring an important competitive advantage to its portfolio companies.

Whitney Rockley on Success

Trust: Firm reliance on the integrity, ability or character of a person

Team: a group organized to work together

Chemistry: the nature and effects of any complex phenomenon

Trust, teamwork and chemistry grows exponentially as an entrepreneur goes from securing love money to angel money to venture capital funding to debt financing to private equity funding. Let's face it, friends and family already love you or they wouldn't give you money. They normally stay out of your way – they are typically silent investors unless you ask them to get involved.

Angels have a soft underbelly for entrepreneurs. They have been successful and they hate being micromanaged so they tend to also be fairly hands off unless they need to rear their heads when venture capitalists enter the scene and potentially dilute them. More so than love money, they will also get involved and help if you ask.

Venture capitalists typically take minority stakes but like to bring in other venture capital investors they know, trust and work well with them. Venture capital investors are hands on, ego-centric, some may say are creative but all will say are in-your-face.

Debt providers can save the day but can also take your company down in one foul swoop. They do not inherently trust the entrepreneur – that is why they ask for security and covenants. A few (and I have experienced this) can be fair and responsive but be wary of the providers that you or your team does not already have a relationship with.

If you have managed to attract mid-market private equity investors, you are off to the races. These guys are the real McCoy's. They take majority positions. They micro-manage. They develop detailed 100-day plans and expect you to stick to them. They are aggressive and hopefully drive you to be more profitable than you already are.

The message is simple. Know your investors before they invest. Speed date your potential investors relentlessly. Talk to people who know them. Do reference checks just like they do reference checks on you. Go skiing or hiking with them to see how they operate outside of the board room. Constantly gauge the chemistry because once they invest, you are committed and just pray to God you are committed in a positive way.

So here's a story for you.....

We backed a guy that was a first time CEO. He first approached a fellow venture capitalist when he was working out of his house. He was too early for venture investment so the CEO found love money and angel investors. Without these early investors he would not be in business. Eventually he moved out of his home and secured an office and had generated just shy of $1 million in revenue. The time was ripe to reach out to the venture capital community again.

I still remember the call I received from my fellow venture capitalist, who is now my partner. He called and said "Whit, I have a hot one for you!" I had looked at companies with this investor over the course of five years. We worked well together and I trusted his judgment.

When I received the call I was working at a large energy company and was responsible for investing in companies that were developing products that were strategic to our business. After this venture capitalist and CEO walked me through the pitch, I was intrigued. The solution solved a pain point in our business so I brought in the right team from my organization to assess the opportunity and we got it done.

Initially I was being brought into the investment opportunity because a couple of other venture capitalists that were looking at the opportunity did not gel with the CEO. The chemistry was off so the CEO decided to sever ties before he took their money.

I get asked a lot, "how do you know when you have chemistry"? It's a hard question to answer. When you feel it, you know it. Chemistry is based on gut instinct and spending a lot of time with people in different scenarios with varying degrees of stress to see how people react. During the due diligence period, which normally lasts for two to three months, it's important to assess and re-assess how well you think you will work with your investors and other members of the team.

The chemistry was good between the CEO and the new investor group. I liked the CEO and so did my fellow co-investors. He had tenacity. He was well respected in the industry. He was passionate and a born leader. He had the "it" factor we all look for in CEOs.

Once the term sheet was signed, the CEO will say that we never once went back to the terms. The venture capitalist that brought me into the company became the chairman of *the board and took the company from less than $1 million in revenue to a run rate of $60 million (prior to going public). The company went public and everyone prospered. But how did we do it?*

Simple.

We worked together as a team. Some of us had worked together. Some of us hadn't but we figured it out. We went through the journey of growing the business quarter-over-quarter. We walked through the wilderness together.

We came out on top.

We trusted each other.

One of the board members said that the CEO was like a freight train. You could not manage him but you could remove barriers in his way so he could steam ahead at full speed. We trusted him to do the right thing. He trusted us, especially when we said that it was time to go public.

Chemistry is something that you have or you don't. We were lucky because we had it.

Trust + Team + Chemistry = Success.

Believe in it. Find it. Live it.

Whitney Rockley
Partner
McRock Capital
www.mcrockcapital.com

About Whitney Rockley, McRock Capital

Rockley brings over 15 years of investment, operating and strategic planning experience in the power, water and Oil & Gas industries. Prior to co-founding McRock Capital, she was a Partner with Emerald Technology Ventures and Nomura New Energy & Clean Technology Ventures. She has extensive experience setting up and managing corporate venture capital programs for large energy and water companies. Rockley previously served as a Director of the Pressure Pipe Inspection Company (acquired by Pure Technologies TSX:PUR), Senscient, TerraLUX, DeepFlex, SpectraSensors (observer), Novinium, and ARXX as well as being an early investor in RuggedCom (TSX:RCM), Silicon Energy (acquired by Itron) and Capstone (NASDAQ: CPST).

In addition to her venture capital experience, Rockley has extensive operating experience in the areas of analytics, finance and environment. Having worked in London, Zurich, San Francisco, Calgary and Toronto, she has an impressive global network.

About McRock Capital

McRock Capital was co-founded by venture capital veterans Scott MacDonald and Whitney Rockley, both of whom have spent their careers investing and building technology companies in the power, water and oil & gas industries. As we enter an era where technology is needed to maximize efficiency because we simply need to do more with less, McRock was founded on the principle that it's fun to work with passionate, intelligent and insanely determined people and it's even more contagious to win alongside of them. Especially when winning means commercializing incredible products and services that customer's desire and, quite frankly, our planet needs.

Mike Satterfield on Pitching

It's hard for entrepreneurs to get a sense of just how tough the competition is to get his or her deal done in a typical VC firm. First, you are competing with hundreds of other entrepreneurs to get the time and attention of the right partner to move your deal forward. And since VC firms want to invest in the best, and best-fit, opportunities the firm is able to attract, that often means a head-to-head comparison with other high-potential opportunities being considered for admission to the firm's investment portfolio.

Much has been written about how to tell your story, and while there clearly remains ample room for improvement, there really isn't a "right" or "best" way. However, if there was a single piece of advice I could give entrepreneurs regarding their pitch, it would be to work as hard to differentiate their investment opportunity from the competition as they would to differentiate their product offering. In other words, know what the key selling point(s) of your opportunity are, in what order, and put the emphasis there. If you don't know what "features" of your deal are most important, your prospective investors might not be able to figure it out either.

So what will move your opportunity to the top of our deal flow stack? Like most firms, we review many opportunities every year, and each of us sits in on a few pitches every week. The ones that get under my skin invariably have something special that really stands out. Good presenters understand the essence of their opportunity, and they know how to emphasize it for maximum effect in their pitch.

My partners and I often talk about whether something is a "technology bet" or a "team bet" or a "traction bet". What we mean is that one aspect of the opportunity is particularly noteworthy, and in identifying the "bet", they are putting their partners on notice that they should pay special attention to this aspect of the deal. Whatever your company's "bet" is, it needs to be remarkable, and as such it should be front and center in your pitch. Conversely, if you tell us some aspect of the company is exemplary and we don't think it's really all that special relative to other things we're looking at, then that's going to be a turn off. So what's your bet?

It has frequently been said that investors will pick an "A" team with a "B" technology over the reverse every time. So if you really do have an "A" team, you should bring that to the fore. Why is this team with this track record exactly right to go after this opportunity. It's not that the other factors don't matter. It's just that the strength of the team is the primary consideration in a team bet. Having heard about the importance investors place on teams, entrepreneurs often put the team right up front in their pitch. But explicitly or implicitly positioning the team as the most important "feature" only works if the team truly is world class, and that usually means a track record of success for these people, working together, in comparable circumstances. It's not that we won't back unproven teams, but it's unlikely that we'll do so as a "team bet".

Since there aren't all that many "A" teams with VC track records out there, what else gets our attention? For unproven teams, it's hard to beat customer traction as the focal point of your pitch. Startups that are winning business from diligent and demanding enterprise customers will almost always get a closer look from us, as will consumer-focused businesses experiencing rapid growth in user acquisition and engagement. Of course we're interested in your vision for your company, but talking about real customers and real *metrics brings the opportunity down to earth for us, and it shows that — even if you haven't yet established your entrepreneurial track record — on this opportunity you have figured out how to execute where it really matters. For these "traction bet" opportunities, an injection of investor cash will enable you to recruit the seasoned talent you'll need to take full advantage of the market beachhead you've already established.*

Where does technology fit into the picture? We absolutely do get excited about game-changing technologies, and we look closely at "technology bet" opportunities. Just be aware that the bar is really high here — while just about everyone these days claims their technology is disruptive, in our view most technology is evolutionary, not revolutionary. But if you do have a proprietary technology that can set a new standard for price/performance in your market, then by all means make that the cornerstone of your pitch. You don't even need to tell us much about how you do it at this stage — we can and do suspend disbelief long enough to hear your story. However, be sure to quantify what you have achieved. And above all, tell us why your technical achievement more than offsets all of the disadvantages buying from a startup entails. So what about the rest of the pitch — like market, strategy, finance etc.? Clearly, they are all important and should be covered to some degree. My point is that you want to take your best shot. By definition, that means you can't give the same emphasis to everything. Put your key selling points into your pitch, push those points hard, get through the rest of the required content promptly, and be ready to address the questions that will naturally flow if you've done your job, which is to set the hook for the next, more detailed, discussion.

Mike Satterfield
Partner
Yaletown Venture Partners
www.yaletown.com

About Mike Satterfield, Yaletown Venture Partners

Mike is a founding Partner of Yaletown Venture Partners. He has over 25 years of entrepreneurial and senior operating experience in the software industry. Mike serves on the boards of Yaletown's portfolio companies Indicee and Partnerpedia and manages Yaletown's investment in GrowLab. Mike has built product development and management teams in Canada and the US, devised and executed business plans, established strategic partnerships, raised venture capital from US and Canadian investors, and participated in the sale of two companies he founded. Prior to co-founding Yaletown, Mike was CEO of Simba Technologies (acquired by Pivotal). Prior to that he co-founded Paradigm Development, a Vancouver-based contract software development firm whose client roster included Microsoft, Adobe and Symantec. Mike has a B.Sc. degree from the University of British Columbia.

About Yaletown Venture Partners

Yaletown Venture Partners, a preferred venture partner for entrepreneurs, angels, syndicate VCs and Limited Partners, is headquartered in Vancouver, Canada with offices on Calgary and Seattle. Yaletown is backed by leading institutional investors in Canada and the United States, and by a network of successful technology entrepreneurs, executives, and angel investors. Yaletown leverages an extensive on-the-ground network to seek out the most promising early stage cleantech and information technology companies in Western Canada and the US Pacific Northwest.

Founded in 2002, Yaletown is led by a team that brings together an extensive network of industry relationships and more than 120 years collective experience building and financing emerging technology companies.

Geoff Smart, Ph.D. on Talent

In the 1992 and 1996 Olympic Games, the American basketball Dream Team had no problem crushing its competitors. What was the primary source of its competitive advantage? Better strategic thinking? Better business processes? Was the team a learning organization? Was it the team's commitment to embrace change and innovation? No. The dream team's fundamental competitive advantage was clearly the talent. All other advantages flowed from this primary driver of performance. The team was comprised of high-performers, or A players. There were almost no B players and certainly no C players to drag the organization's talent level down.

AlliedSignal's Chairman and CEO Larry Bossidy is a believer that nothing his company does is more important than hiring and developing the right people. He contends that strategies are intellectually simple but the success of strategy implementation depends on who is doing the implementing. Proactively seeking out and employing the most talented people can have a multiplier effect on the creation of other competitive advantages. High-performers, the A players, contribute more, innovate more, work smarter, earn more trust, display more resourcefulness, take more initiative, develop better business strategies, implement change more effectively, deliver higher quality work, demonstrate greater teamwork, and find ways to get the job done in less time with less cost. Across our sample of companies, only 25% of their employees were A players, 55% were B players, and 20% were C players.

What is topgrading?

Topgrading simply means proactively seeking out and employing the most talented people available, while redeploying (internally or externally) those of lesser ability or performance. More specifically, we view topgrading as employing only A players. These folks are in the top 10% of the talent available. "Available" is defined as the total number of people in the pool of talent who are willing to work for a given compensation level, in a given company, in a given town. Whether the number of available people is 20 or 20,000, topgrading means inserting only the most talented ones available into every job. B players fall in the next lower 25%, and C players drop below the 65th percentile. In fact, dozens of competencies should be included, and they should be carefully tailored to the specific job.

Another way of thinking about top-grading is making a commitment to realizing the most "bang for one's buck" with respect to the total cost to employ people. The process of topgrading should start with the board's decision to topgrade the CEO. Unlike so many factors that also affect shareholder value, the board and senior management can directly control the talent level of the company.

Geoff Smart, Ph.D.
Chairman &CEO
ghSMART
www.ghsmart.com

About Geoff Smart, Ph.D., ghSMART

Geoff Smart is a CEO, bestselling author, and social entrepreneur whose mission is to create, communicate, and put into practice useful ideas about leadership. Geoff serves as Chairman & CEO of ghSMART. ghSMART is a leadership firm for CEOs and investors, which Geoff founded in 1995. The firm was named one the "world's top firms" in Broderick's The Art of Managing Professional Services, and is the subject of two Harvard Business School Cases titled "ghSMART & Co.: Pioneering in Professional Services." Geoff is co-author, with his colleague Randy Street, of the New York Times bestselling book Who: The A Method for Hiring. The book is one of the bestselling and most-acclaimed books in the world on the topic of hiring leaders, which The Wall Street Journal calls "the most important aspect of business." Soundview Executive Book Summaries gave Who the "Best 30 Business Books Award." Shanghai Daily named it a "Top 5 Business Book in China." Canada's Globe and Mail named Who the "#1 Best Business and Management Book of 2009." Geoff is also co-creator of the Topgrading® philosophy of talent management.

As a social entrepreneur, Geoff is Chairman and Co-founder of SMARTKids Leadership Program™, a 501c3 not-for-profit foundation. It provides a customized program of 10 years of leadership mentoring and a $100,000 scholarship to top students with leadership potential from low-income communities. He is Chairman and Founder of THE LEADERS INITIATIVE™, whose mission is to elevate humanity by identifying, developing, and deploying society's greatest leaders into government. Geoff and his ghSMART colleagues also provide pro bono leadership advisory services to leaders in the fields of education, healthcare, and government.

Geoff earned a B.A. in Economics with Honors from Northwestern University, an M.A., and a Ph.D. in Psychology with emphasis in Leadership from Claremont Graduate University, where he was a student of Peter F. Drucker. He was elected to Sigma Xi, the honorary society for holders of doctoral degrees, and is a member of Young Presidents' Organization (YPO).

About ghSMART

ghSMART is the management assessment firm for CEOs and investors. Founded in 1995, our mission has always been to use our expertise in human behavior to help CEOs and investors build valuable companies. ghSMART is the brand of trusted advisor that helps clients answer their most important business questions. These are questions not of "what", but of "who." We are able to achieve very high client satisfaction by leveraging our team of talented experts in human behavior (1 in 500 applicants to ghSMART is hired), our proprietary branded methods (featured in a Harvard Business School case study), and the largest relevant database in existence of CEO and investor performance (a database described as "coveted" by the Wall Street Journal 11/19/2007). We specialize in management assessment for pre-hire decisions at the CEO and board levels, private equity and corporate M&A management due diligence, M&A integration, CEO succession, board effectiveness, organizational performance improvement, senior management team performance feedback, and executive learning and development to maximize career success and financial performance.

Mike Volker on Deal Terms

If you are very bright, very tenacious, and financially well endowed, then you can start a company which you own in its entirety and in which you can hire a bright, capable, highly motivated and well-paid management team. However, if you do not fit this description entirely (I might add that, if you do not possess at least one of these attributes, you might want to re-think starting your own business), then you will likely have to bring "partners" into your company by giving them equity, i.e. some share ownership. Obviously, investors who bring money to fuel the growth of your company deserve some ownership. Similarly, key people who join you on your team, or who start the company with you, will want some form of ownership if they are making a valuable contribution for which they are not being fully paid in cash. Others who contribute their skills, experience, ideas, or other assets (such as intellectual property) may be given shares in your company in lieu of being paid in cash.

Valuation is the issue. What is the new partner's contribution worth in relation to the whole pie? At that moment in time, what is the company worth and how is that worth determined? Bringing in new shareholders always means "dilution" to the existing shareholders. If a new investor is to receive a 10% stake in the company, then a shareholder who previously held 40% of the equity, will now hold 36% (i.e. 90% of 40%). You never actually never give up your shares when new people are dealt in. You simply issue more shares (the same way governments print money). Issuing more shares is what causes the dilution. If you have 100 shares and you want to give someone 10%, you'd have to issue 11 new shares (11/111 x 100 = 10%, approximately).

Unless you are greatly concerned about control issues, each time you dilute you should be increasing your economic value. If you dilute your ownership from 40% to 36%, you still hold the same number of shares, but the per-share value should have increased. If you bring in a new VP of Marketing and give her 5% as a signing bonus, how do you know that her contribution will be worth 5%? How do you measure someone's reputation? Unless the person is well known or has a proven record, it may not be so easy. That's why vesting (described later) may be appropriate. There is only one way to bring in new partners: carefully and with deliberation. A partner may be with you for life. It may be more difficult to terminate a business partnership than it is to obtain a marital divorce. So think about it!

Who Should Get What?

What percentage of the company should each partner in a new venture receive? This is a tough question for which there is no easy answer. In terms of percentage points, what's an idea (or invention or patent) worth? What's 5 years of low salary, sweat and intense commitment worth? What is experience and know-how worth? What's a buck worth? "Who should get what" is best determined by considering who brings what to the table.

Suppose Bill Gates said he'd serve on your Board or give you some help. What share of the company should he get? Just think about the value that his name would bring to your company! If a venture capitalist thought your company was worth $1 million without Gates, that value would increase several-fold with Gates' involvement. Yet, what has he "done" for you?

Often, company founders give little thought to this question. In many cases, the numbers are determined by what "feels good", i.e. gut-feeling. For example, in the case of a brand-

new venture started from scratch by four engineers, the tendency might be to share equally in the new deal at 25% each. In the case of a single founder, that person may choose to keep 100% of the shares and build this venture through a "bootstrapping" process, in order to maintain total ownership and control by not dealing in other partners. It may be possible to defer dealing in new partners until some later time at which point the business has some inherent value thereby allowing the founder to maintain a substantial ownership position.

The answer to the question "who should get what" is, in principle, simple to answer: It depends on the relative contributions and commitments made to the company by the partners at that moment in time. Therefore, it is necessary to come up with a value for the company, expressed in either monetary terms or some other common denominator. It gets trickier when there are hard assets (cash, equipment) contributed by some parties and soft assets (intellectual property, know-how) contributed by others. Let's look at a some examples for illustration.

1. Professor Goldblum has developed a new product for decreasing the cost of automobile fuel consumption. He decides that in order to bring this innovation to market, he will need a business partner to help him with a business plan, and then manage and finance a new company formed to exploit this opportunity. He recruits Sam Brown, aged 45, who has a good record as a local entrepreneur. They agree that Sam will get 30% of the company for contributing his experience, contacts, and track record plus the fact that he will take a $50K/year salary instead of a "market" salary of $100K for the first two years. Furthermore, they agree that Sam will commit his full-time attention to the firm for 5 years and that should he leave, for whatever reason before the full term, he would forfeit 4% of the equity for each year under the 5 year term. The Professor takes 60% for *contributing the intellectual property and for providing on-going technical advice and support. The Professor "gives" the University a token 10% because according to University policy, the University is entitled to "some share" of his intellectual property because of its contribution of facilities even though, under its policy, the intellectual property rights rest with the creator. Although these numbers are somewhat arbitrary, they are seen by the parties as being fair based on the relative contributions of the parties.*

2. Three freshly graduated software engineers decide to form a new software company which will develop and sell a suite of software development tools, bearing in mind the paucity of software talent plaguing the industry. They all start off with similar assets, i.e. knowledge of software, and comparable contributions of "sweat equity". Heidi takes on the role of CEO of the new venture and they divide the pie as to 40% for Heidi (because of her greater responsibilities) and 30% each for the other two. They are happy campers for now. Sometime later, they decide to recruit a seasoned CEO with relevant experience and bring in a Venture Capital investor to fund the promotion of their then-developed and shippable suite of software products. They will then have to wrestle with the issue of what their company is now worth and how much ownership they will have to trade for these new resources. This will be determined by the venture capital suitor(s) in light of current market investment conditions and the attractiveness of this particular deal.

3. Four entrepreneurs who have recently enjoyed financial windfalls from their businesses, decide to get into the venture capital business. They decide to form a company with $10 million in investment capital. Harry provides $3 million, Bill provides $2 million, and the other two each provide $2.5 million. How much of the new company will each of them own? (This isn't a trick question.) For assets as basic as cash, it is easy to determine "fair" percentages.

In the case of the second example above, we have a situation in which a company is established and has some value by virtue of its products and potential sales in the market. The company's Board decides to bring in an experienced CEO (this also makes the venture capitalist happy) to develop the business to its next stage of growth. Although it may be possible to hire such a person and pay him/her an attractive salary, it probably makes more sense to bring in such a person as more of a partner than a hired hand. In this case a lower-than-market salary could be negotiated along with an equity stake. One way of doing this is to apply the difference between market rate and the actual salary over a period of time, say 5 years, to an equity position based on a company valuation acceptable to the founders. If a venture capital investment has been made or is being negotiated, this may set the stage for such a valuation. For example, Louise was earning $125,000 per year working as the CEO of an American company's Canadian operations. She agrees to work for $75,000 per year for 5 years. She is essentially contributing $250,000 up front (in the form of equity that does not have to be raised to hire her). If the company has been valued at $2 million, she ought to receive something in excess of 10% of the company. However, her shares would "vest" over 5 years meaning that each year she would receive one-fifth of the shares from "escrow". She would forfeit any shares not so released should she break her commitment or should her employment be terminated for cause. In this example, Louse's salary is really $125,000 per year but she is investing a portion of this in the company's equity (on a tax-advantaged basis, I might add!).

What's a Company Worth? (and When?)

How is value added to a business over a period of time? All companies start off being worth only the incorporation expense. As soon as people, money and assets are added or developed, a company will appreciate in value. If the management team comes up with a breakthrough technology, that may be worth millions of dollars! The development of products and customers adds value. The management team itself is worth something by virtue of its aggregate experience, skill, contacts, etc. Value is best measured in terms of potential, not in terms of historical earnings or financial track record - but in terms of future performance possibilities. Value increases both through internal actions and growth as well as through external contributions (e.g. cash and people) which facilitate such growth.

For founders and early investors, the upside potential is the greatest. In its early stages of development a company may be worth very little, especially to outsiders. All of the value may be dormant within the team - awaiting development. Those who contribute at this early stage deserve to enjoy enormous gains because they are the ones who are bold enough to take the initial risks. An "angel" investor who provides a University faculty member with a small amount of start-up funding, say $50,000 to prepare an invention for exploitation, may easily deserve 10 or 20% of that business. After a concept is more fully developed, this initial position may be viewed as a "steal", but then again, most such "steals" end up being worthless deals!

It is both unhealthy and unrealistic for an entrepreneur to begrudge the stake held by his or her early backers. Sometimes there is a tendency towards seller's remorse. For example, an entrepreneur who sells 20% of his firm for $50,000 may feel cheated one year hence when a serious investor is willing to pay $500,000 for 20%. This is flawed thinking. Without that initial $50,000, this company may never have survived its first year. In this illustration, the founder initially had 100%, then 80%, then ended up with 64%. The angel had 20%, then ended up with 16%. The rich investor ended up with 20% -

at least until the next round at which time they will all again suffer a dilution. Ideally, as time marches on, the value of the company increases dramatically such that subsequent dilutions become less and less painful to existing stakeholders. Sometimes, when milestones are not achieved, the early investors and founders must swallow a bitter pill by enticing new investors with large equity positions with major dilutive consequences. But, that's business!

The value of a business is best ascertained by what an investor is willing to pay for it (i.e. its shares) or what a potential strategic acquisitor (i.e. an investor (or competitor) who wants to buy it for strategic business reasons) is willing to pay for it.

It is prudent management philosophy to always be thinking in terms of making a business attractive to such suitors by building a solid foundation and by nurturing and growing it. The business should always be in a condition to sell.

Dividing the pie is not easy. In the end, or to put it more correctly - in the beginning, it is important that all equity partners accept the deal. At the time you sell some or all of your shares in the company, remember that it is dollars which you put into your bank account, not percentage points.

Mike Volker
Angel Investor
mikevolker.com

About Mike Volker

Michael Volker is an Entrepreneur active in the development of new high technology ventures. A University of Waterloo Engineering grad, Mike started his own company (Volker-Craig Ltd) in 1973. He sold this company in 1981 and then decided to work with entrepreneurs in building new companies. He is presently the director of Simon Fraser University's Innovation Office. Check out his latest two projects: Greenangel Energy Corp, [GAE.V] a public company that invests in green technologies and WUTIF - the Western Universities Technology Innovation Fund - an "angel" fund for start-ups. To further encourage tech entrepreneurship, Mike runs the Vancouver Angel Network, VANTEC and he's also quite active with New Ventures BC - an annual business competition. Mike was also chairman of the Vancouver Enterprise Forum for several years.

ABOUT THE AUTHOR

Warren Bergen is an award-winning entrepreneur, investor, corporate advisor and has directly raised or assisted in the capital raise for many growing businesses. He has participated directly with early stage ventures for over 15 years and has raised growth capital from venture capitalists, accredited investors, private equity groups and public markets. He was the Executive Director of Alberta Deal Generator, a network of venture capitalists, private equity and angel investors in Calgary and Edmonton, Alberta. He is a former board member of the National Angel Capital Organization and has participated as a guest lecturer and panelist at many investment conferences. He is currently Vice President, Corporate Development, AVAC Ltd., a company that has invested over $100Million in promising early-stage businesses in agri-value, ICT, life science, and other industrial technology sectors.

* * * * *

The Entrepreneur

Apart from constant restlessness,

we're truly quite content.

We strive hard for whiteboard goals in bold,

and aspire to far beyond.

The clarity of what will be,

grants allowance for the pains of now.

Escaping a grind, we've taken a leap,

and occasionally kick at doubt.

A captivating place to be,

but it's always hard to sleep.

* * * * *

Made in the USA
Lexington, KY
13 April 2013